Praise for AMERICAN MUSLIM
An Immigrant's Journey

American Muslim captures a remarkable odyssey of an audacious woman, an immigrant, a mother and a brilliant leader. It's powerful and honest. It reminds us all what it means to be an American, how it's up to each and every one of us to make America meet its promise and ambition, no matter where we came from, no matter where we work or where we pray. Saima's writing is captivating and engaging. It's a beautiful memoir, nuanced and honest. In this book, you will learn a lot of things: about American Islam, about being a first-generation immigrant, about being a mom and a good neighbor. And if you read carefully, I guarantee it — you will learn a few things about yourself. I know I did.

> — *Mila Sanina, executive director and editor of PublicSource.org*

A profoundly honest account of the immigrant experience that confronts preconceived notions heads on. It never idolizes or vilifies either the culture left behind or the newly adopted one but looks for a gracious and graceful understanding of both. You'll fall in love with the narrator as she discovers herself.

> — *Kornelia Tancheva, Ph.D., The Hillman University librarian and director of the University Library System, University of Pittsburgh*

Saima's memoir, American Muslim, captures autobiographical details of her life, as an educated, professional girl from Pakistan who migrated as a married woman to the United States of America. The vivid descriptions of the initial difficulties that she faced make an interesting read. The book also details racial disparities systemically rooted in the American society. Motivated by her desire to be part of the movement to do social good, Saima has found her calling in building bridges across identities and cultures.

> — *Sayeed Hasan Khan, former BBC journalist, author and a social activist who marched on Washington in 1963, with Martin Luther King Jr.*

American Muslim written by Saima Adil Sitwat illustrates the process of cultural assimilation of an immigrant in the New World. The landscape of this journey is painted with the brilliant choices of otherwise minor events selected with deep observation. The journey of a physician's young wife begins with a Karachi- Chicago flight in 2003. Gradually unfolded are the family's bright and hazy days, which are a delight to read. Sitwat writes with sensitivity the struggle with sweet memories of her old home and contrasts it with the loneliness of the new home. Depressive and jolly, the high and low swings of life are depicted with keen insight. As our narrator exchanges her place in life— from a humble library volunteer to a graduate student at the University of Pittsburgh, she meets limitless possibilities of the American dream - one of them becoming the first woman president of one of Pittsburgh's leading mosques. Sitwat's prose is straightforward, concise, fluid and engaging. It is difficult to put the book down and it's well- worth the read. *American Muslim* will warm your heart and fill in a much-needed void in immigrants' stories.

> — *S. Shaukat Ali Zaidi, Pakistani- Canadian author, essayist and poet*

Saima's story is the story of her own experiences, her own voice. But it is also a story of common heartbreaks, common jolts of happiness, and the hope, and pride, that ties all of us to each other. 2020 has been a year for awakenings, none all that great, but all necessary. At the heart of these communal awakenings is the belief that diversity is not to be feared of but to be celebrated. It is not a weakness but is the only form of strength we need to survive. And, in this diverse country, until we start treating each other as equals none of us will be truly free. Saima's story of her life in the U.S., her education in *Americanization, her continuous struggle to learn, unlearn, and relearn, her daily inner struggle to juggle her multiple roles and responsibilities,* truly show immigration to the United States of America is not for the faint of heart. It takes constant effort, endless perseverance, and yet remains fragile and can be broken by a slight comment of a coworker or a neighbor. Saima's story illustrates how the definition of a migrant in the textbooks as one "seeking permanent residency outside the country of origin" is truly understated. Through her story, as much as our own, we affirm that 'origin' is anything but one single place. And, that is a really good thing for all of us.

— *Dr. Müge Finkel, Graduate School for Public and International Affairs (GSPIA), University of Pittsburgh*

AMERICAN MUSLIM

AN IMMIGRANT'S JOURNEY

For Bilal,

for having faith in me, even at times, when I did not have faith in myself.

CONTENTS

AUTHOR'S NOTE

All events and conversations in the book are recollected to the best of my abilities. To protect people's privacy, I have modified some names.

English translations of the Arabic and Urdu vocabulary highlighted in italics can be found in the glossary at the end, in alphabetical order.

PROLOGUE

"Even when it's not pretty or perfect. Even when it's more real than you want it to be. Your story is what you have, what you will always have. It is something to own."

-Michelle Obama, Becoming

The year was 2003. I stepped outside on my apartment's patio to get a feel of temperatures outside. The chill in the Chicago air on that November afternoon seemed odd. I rechecked the temperature on the weather channel to make sure that it was 30 degrees outside. It was 30 degrees, indeed. I stepped outside, without a jacket, placing my trust in the numbers.

The windchill hit me as soon as I stepped out. Karachi, my native city by the sea, in the South of Pakistan, was never so cold when the temperatures neared 30 degrees. My first week in the United States of America, I stood with folded arms and puzzled eyes on South Ashland Avenue in Chicago's Medical District. I observed people bundled up in parkas and scarves, their heads down, walking fast to avoid the cold. Those who dared to brave shards of chill air in their eyes looked at me with curiosity and surprise. I stood, a South Asian damsel, dressed in *shalwar kameez*, without a piece of warm clothing

1

on myself, bewildered by this contrast in the numbers and sensation of weather. It took me at least a week to recognize that all 30 degrees were not the same.

My husband of six months, Bilal, a medical resident at that time, would leave home all bundled up like other folks, during early hours of the morning, and did not return until late at night. A demanding call schedule at Sinai Children's Hospital in Chicago required him to stay the night at the hospital every other day. It was not until the following Saturday that Bilal and I could go out together. As my husband stuffed himself into gloves, hat, boots, scarf and an oversized coat, he looked puzzled at my attire of choice:

"Aren't you going to be cold without a jacket?" He asked with astonishment.

The conversation that ensued was my first lesson in "Americanism." What I thought of as 30 °C was actually 30 °F. Henceforth, I was to read temperatures in Fahrenheit and not Celsius. For the first twenty-three years of my life, 30 degrees had meant heat and humidity. From now on, it was going to stand for subzero temperatures. That was something I had never experienced in my then limited existence.

That first year in Chicago, I became a student of "Americanism." On this journey, I had to unlearn and relearn. My first lesson was in English. I used to teach college-level English in Pakistan, but it was wholly different in Illinois. In later years, one of my friends from Rwanda would say, "We come here speaking English. But American is another language!"

I would learn that something that would light my way in the dark is a "flashlight" and not a "torch." The latter has a more destructive purpose and therefore should never be asked for, especially if you are Muslim. An alarm does not sound or ring but "goes off" and my favorite vegetable was called "okra" and not ladyfinger in my new homeland. As the years went by, I learned that a good life is "dope," you have a crush on a "hot" not a "cool" guy and "lit" is not short for literature. I learned to ask for "cream" and not "milk" for my coffee. As an English major in college, I had always loved to learn new words. This was pretty fun for me! What was more frustrating and often drew me to tears were the accents. In the city of Chicago, everyone seemed to speak English their own way. From the local Blacks and Midwesterners to Italians, Polish, East and South Asians who had come to inhabit this city like myself from different parts of the world, all had their own versions of English. In two years, we would move to Pittsburgh and I would have to learn "Pittsburghese," as part of my baptism into the city.

And then there was the American culture. It was overtly gregarious and preposterously extroverted, where people of opposite genders shook hands and hugged each other, all the time. It was hard for me to get accustomed to it. I came from a place where even husbands refrained from showing outwardly symbols of affection to their wives in public. In my native country, at times walking alongside your spouse would be considered inappropriate. While shaking and holding hands was a faux pas in Pakistan, hugging between members of the opposite genders was culturally forbidden. Pakistani culture, rooted in the Islamic values of modesty and the South Asian influence of separation between genders, did not encourage any physical interaction between members of the opposite sexes even if they were close or blood relatives.

But America was a different story. As I learned American vocabulary, my body language also had to change. Men and women shook hands out of respect but hugged each other as a show of warmth. For the formative years of my life, hugging a man had only signified romantic inclination but here in the United States, it did not even mean displaying affection. It was just a way of greeting.

I hoped to graduate with a degree in "Americanism" in a year, but

3

am still waiting for a diploma, seventeen years down the line. Along the way, I became a homemaker, a mother, a graduate student, a writer and a community organizer. I learned the American stereotypes of Oreo, Banana and Towelhead. I also consciously recognized and learned to confront my own biases that I had carried all the way from Pakistan with myself.

And I truly appreciate the electric switches marked with on and off, as my muscle memory continues to acclimatize to switching them in the right direction, which used to be the opposite of it in my earlier life.

. 1 .

FRESH OFF THE PLANE

"The world in which you were born is just one model of reality. Other cultures are not failed attempts at being you; they are unique manifestations of the human spirit."

-Wade Davis, writer, photographer and explorer

It all started with cleaning the bathroom.

I had never seen or experienced anything in my life of twenty-three years until then, like those first few days at the Medical District City Apartments building in Chicago. I was born and brought up in a multigenerational home in Pakistan, which meant living in an expansive house with grandparents, aunts, uncles and frequent guests. Our household, like all upper middle-income families in Pakistan, was maintained by an army of domestic help. At home, women cooked out of love, not necessity. A family of maids would come every day to clean our multistory house and spent a great part of the day dusting, cleaning and mopping the premises.

Bilal was on call the day I arrived in the United States. Aftab *bhai,* a dear family friend, who would later become my lifeline during our stay in Chicago, picked me up from the O'Hare airport. He dropped me off at our apartment building, with a caution against consuming anything that was in the refrigerator. Chances were that Bilal was still eating the food cooked by Aftab bhai's mother a couple of weeks earlier and I may not want to gamble my health the very first day in the US.

My jet lag after almost a day of travelling was terrible. As soon as I arrived at my lonely apartment, I crashed on the bed, by which I mean one of the two mattresses I saw on the living room floor. Bilal returned home at some late hour of night, when I was fast asleep. He had left Pakistan earlier in November to join his medical residency program and we had not seen each other in three weeks.

Finally, we met and talked at 4 a.m. in the morning. My young husband looked sleepy, tired and exhausted. Navigating bus and metro routes had consumed his life. He seemed bewildered by different standards at his workplace for locals and immigrants. We would later know that this discrimination was pervasive in American society at multiple levels. People born in America judged immigrants, while immigrants prided themselves over native born for making it in America. White immigrants judged the nonwhite ones, and brown-skinned people like me could often be heard talking about white fragility. It seemed as if everyone judged, or misjudged, the Black community. Today, after seventeen years of living in the United States, my husband still recalls a time when his team covering the hospital floor one night was ordering dinner. Bilal wanted to order a Big Mac from McDonalds and was told off by a nurse, "Just because you are in the US, doesn't mean that you have to eat McDonalds." At another time, he had to hear that he had different "cultural expectations," while his workplace tried to cover for the slacking off of another employee.

Both Bilal and I had grown up as the *Sunni Muslim* majority in Pakistan, and were unaccustomed to how minority communities around the world, including those in Pakistan, normalized slurs and stereotypes attached to them. Over a period of years, it would become our habit to overlook racist and anti-immigrant remarks, made by others with a casual flair.

On that first day in Chicago, as Bilal left for work in the early hours of the morning, I turned attention to my surroundings. Our one-bedroom apartment was "furnished" with two single mattresses, a plastic folding table with four chairs, two lamps and a desk. We had acquired these items, courtesy of Bilal's new friend and fellow resident, Thomas Bockle, and his church. There was food in the refrigerator that I was already advised to dispose of. There was an appliance in the kitchen that I had never seen before. It was called a dishwasher.

The bathroom commanded my immediate attention. It looked like a place in need of a good scrubbing before I could indulge in a shower. I found detergents provided by the leasing company in the medicine cabinet. Charged with the zest of becoming a super-housewife on my first day at duty, I tried to remember how I had seen maids back home clean the bathroom. They always "washed" the bathroom. I filled a bucket of water and trundled water on the floor. I rolled one more bucket. It took three buckets of water for me to realize that the water was not going anywhere and only accumulating in the bathroom. Some of it had started to make its way onto the living room carpet from the opening under the bathroom door.

Panicked, I called Bilal. My double-panicked husband enlightened me that there were no drains in the "American bathrooms," unlike in Pakistan, where every bathroom has two to three drains at different positions to allow smooth flow of water. I had to quickly think of a damage control strategy. For the next few hours, I refilled the bucket with water on the floor, used mop to soak up some water as well, and drained it down the bathtub.

Finally, the bathroom was clean, and I could take a long, luxurious bath.

On that first day in Chicago, as my initiation into a life I wasn't raised to live, I learned the most important skill of self-reliance. This was going to be my life and I was responsible for fixing any screw-ups. I would have many mishaps along the way, but the bathroom and the bucket episode always reminded me of a time when I averted a tsunami that could have destroyed a carpet, I had no money to replace.

It might have been a rough start, but during those first few months of winter and holiday season in Chicago, Bilal and I experienced many firsts together. On our first trip to the supermarket, I was amazed by the choice of cereals and chips. To me, corn flakes were the only kind of cereal and chips came in a yellow bag called potato chips. Here in America, canned and cooked frozen food was cheap and fresh produce was expensive. It was the other way around where I came from. Extenuating finances led us on the path of making unhealthy food choices from the very first day in America. We might not be poor, but were frugal with whatever little money we had. Why would someone pay more to purchase groceries and then cook them too, while on the other hand you could eat them right out of the box? It was not just Bilal and I who gradually over the years headed towards obesity. It has now been established as a fact backed by research that American households who struggle with money are compelled to make unhealthy food choices which puts them on a trajectory towards obesity and related health problems. I would never forget the time when in 2015, one of my administrative coworkers at Allegheny County Department of Human Services told me that she had never seen a full avocado, and only knew it as "the green stuff that goes inside a Subway sandwich for an extra dollar."

During our year of firsts, Bilal and I opened our first bank account at Chase. We chose the bank because it had no penalty for going below $0. We bought our first car, a seven-year-old Geo Prizm, on a generous no-interest loan given by one of Bilal's cousins. We celebrated the first "real" Christmas and also our first *Eid* together. Having grown up in a country, where ninety-nine percent of population was Muslim, Christians comprised a tiny minority within a total of one percent minorities. Though as a student of English Literature, I had fantasized about grand holiday scenes from British classics, my own personal exposure to Christmas was limited to a night of carols, sung in Urdu on the national television, by a few singers of the Anglo-Indian descent in the country.

Bilal worked on both Christmas and *Eid*, not realizing that one could actually request time off for a personal holiday. On weekends, we would go for movies, and would sometimes watch three flicks at a time. The second sequel in the series of the famous trilogy, "The Lord of the Rings: The Return of the King" came out in December 2003. I could not stop boasting to friends back home in Pakistan about having watched the blockbuster on the big screen at AMC Theater in Downtown Chicago.

By Fall 2004, after almost nine months in America, we were ready for the quintessential American experience, which was to undertake a road trip. The plan was to fly to Los Angeles, stay with one of Bilal's distant cousins and then drive for approximately five hours to Las

Vegas to witness "America's finest." Vacation gave us time to discover each other, more so than in the humdrum of life in Chicago. It was great to get out. We went to the Disney Land where I got to know about Bilal's aversion to roller coasters. We shared our fascination for Mickey Mouse and Winnie the Pooh. It was exciting to see and have an all-access pass to experience characters from our childhood who were no more than glimpses for five minutes at a time, during our cable-free childhood in Pakistan. I was equally fascinated by turkey legs. But what really impressed me were the ADA protocols for people with special needs on all the park rides. In the country of my birth, I had rarely come across people with special needs because it was not possible for them to be part of my fully functioning world without any accommodations. It was only during that first trip to Disney Land that I realized the difference that accommodations can make in the quality of a person's life.

On our first night in Los Angeles, Bilal's cousin casually asked about the hotel where we planned to stay in Las Vegas. The question confused us both. We had no idea that making reservations was a thing. Once we learned how hard it was to find a place to stay at the Strip over the weekend, we frantically started checking availability of rooms at hotels available in the next two days. Whatever was available was either sixty miles out of Vegas or as expensive for a night as our apartment's monthly rent. Flabbergasted, we headed out on our road trip without having a room to stay in Vegas. The rocky mountainous terrain between California and Nevada was breathtaking. I never knew that the desert and cacti in the wild could look so beautiful.

We found a room to stay in Mesquite, Nevada, almost by the Arizona state line, eighty miles northeast of Las Vegas. We might have landed in Mesquite through our misfortune, but it was an experience in and of itself. The place was so far removed from the glitter and dazzle of Las Vegas, as the reality of my life in America was from the general Pakistani perception. It was our first time in small town America. The slot machines and noise inside the hotel was in stark contrast to the quite deserted lands outside. It was an alternative universe of peace and tranquility, a place far removed from Vegas in distance and essence.

Our first morning in a Mesquite hotel was an experience in itself. In order to provide entertainment for those who could not find a place to stay on the Strip, because of finances or necessity, the hotel had its own gaming area with slot machines and poker tables. There were no viable restaurants on premises though.

Our only option for breakfast was a lone diner in the neighborhood and diners were some of the places we had been cautioned against trying out by our Pakistani friends. "All diner food has bacon," One of our friends had cautioned us just like another one who had proclaimed; "All Chinese food has pork." Bilal and I had stayed away from both until that time. But there was little available in Mesquite in 2004, except for diners and Chinese buffets.

On that morning in September 2004, we hesitantly entered a diner full of white people. Nobody seemed to notice our presence, but we felt scrutinized, nonetheless. Such were our presumptions and fear of the places unknown! The smiling, matronly server stopped by to take our order. From a jargon of scrambled and sunny-side-up eggs on the menu, the only items that made sense were different kinds of omelets. We were overjoyed to see that we could get a vegetarian one, without bacon. "Would you like some hash with your omelets?" asked our matronly server. "Umm… Hash?" I asked. "Yes- hash browns," she replied. "No. Thank you!" Both Bilal and I responded in unison.

On second thought I asked, "What exactly is hash brown?" "Potato." The server responded with the disbelief of a person who would have to explain potatoes to adults.

"Not bacon?" It was my turn to be surprised. "No, we don't put bacon in our hash. It's just potatoes," retorted the serving lady.

Bilal and I were embarrassed as well as relieved. We enjoyed our first taste of hash brown, which jokes aside, I first thought of as some version of the drug hashish incorporated into a bacon-like composition. Such is the stuff conspiracy theories in the minds of Muslim immigrants are made of! The perception our predecessors had created seemed to be as if the world out there is sneaking pork into our food and alcohol in our drinks.

Our next stop that day was an equally fascinating Chinese buffet. We had tried out Chinese food in Chicago, but a Chinese buffet was a different experience, starkly in contrast with the expensive and formal Chinese restaurants we were used to visiting in our hometown, Karachi. You could eat all that you cared for and it also proved to be educational like the diner in the morning. We realized that Asian folks enjoyed and served meat apart from pork as well. However, to this day Bilal still looks at red peppers in his Chinese food with suspicion, given the pretext that it might be pork.

As the day diffused into night, we drove down twenty miles to the Strip in the city of Las Vegas. It was a different world, far off from the quiet town of Mesquite. Together, we explored Vegas, taking pictures of the magnificent casinos, truly fascinated by the life inside them and outside on the street. We had more Chinese food, this time on the Strip. Vegas, with its splendor, was exciting and disturbing at the same time.

Vegas was fun, but on our first vacation together, Bilal and I got to know so much more about ourselves as a couple as we explored the places we visited together. It hit us that we were more Mesquite than Vegas. The nightlife exhausted us. We wanted to go to bed at midnight and that was just around the time things would be heating up at the Strip.

As I look back at it today, I feel that there was part of us that was scared of Vegas and all that it stood for. Our upbringing in middle-income families in a developing country had taught us to value money in ways that stopped us from "having fun" with it. Gambling was a moral sin in Islam. To see it flow and waste so casually in the gaming capital of the world was frightening. People were betting with their credit cards, while we with our meager paychecks at the time were always consumed by the idea of maintaining a zero debt.

Still, we played a few hands at the slot machines and lucked out. I made $75 out of $2 but eventually lost it all. Out of our three days in Vegas, we spent one full day in Mesquite, deciding against going to the Strip and enjoying our favorite diner and Chinese buffet with a new sense of liberation that only comes with enlightenment. We could have pork free food anywhere we chose to eat- this revelation would turn us into takeout junkies during the years that ensued. We returned refreshed and rejuvenated from our trip. In the days before phone cameras and social media, we took more than 500 pictures with our digital camera and shared pictures with family and friends through the then popular Yahoo pictures. Everyone back home oohed and aahed. To my family and friends in Pakistan, I was living the American Dream.

That was a facade I had worked hard to create. All was not well with me. I came from a family of teachers and educators. A valedictorian of my graduate class, I was offered a job even before I had formally graduated. In Pakistan, I worked as a college teacher at a prestigious girls' college and wrote for the national newspapers. I had achieved my dreams and was on my way to becoming what I had always aspired to be, "an independent woman." However, here in the United States, I was literally a "dependent spouse" on a J-2 visa. The visa allowed employment but with many restrictions and only under a work authorization permit, called Employment Authorization Document (EAD), to be obtained by the United States Citizenship and Immigration Services (USCIS). It required extensive paperwork and $120, which seemed enormous to afford, given our yearly income of less than $40,000. The permit had to be renewed every year with the annual processing of our visa paperwork. My first work permit under J-2 arrived in September 2004 and was to expire in November of the same year. The nuances of visa combined with a tough job market during 2004 that eventually became the Great Recession did not make it easy for me to secure a job.

While I stayed home, I filled my days with homemaking and volunteering at the Harold Washington Public Library in Chicago. I could tell that eventually the librarians also felt bad for me, as I worked diligently for months and months. They wanted to hire me, but could not do so because of the long time my EAD was taking to process.

I would start mornings watching the likes of Jerry Springer and Maury Show and fill up my evenings with back-to-back episodes of Judge Judy, Friends, The Simpsons and That '70s Show. My morning shows were educational in a very profound way and often left me wondering about where and whom my husband was spending time with, while on thirty-six-hour work shifts. Sometimes, I would venture outside and pick up dinner from the neighboring Taylor Street in Chicago's famous Little Italy neighborhood. At other times, I would go down to our apartment building's gym, and work out in my *shalwar kameez*, which by that time I had started using as my PJs. It was a carefree time, full of ignorant bliss. I was not aware of any biases that could be sparked because of how I looked or talked.

However, as the time went by and my honeymoon with America as well as my new husband was over, I grew homesick. I missed the love of my parents, warmth of close family and friends I had grown up with and being surrounded by people who spoke Urdu, my native language. I grew frustrated with less money to spend and more responsibilities to shoulder. The Pakistani women I met during this time did their best to support me with their wisdom and years of experience.

One family, in particular, helped and guided us through indoctrination into the Pakistani-American life. Anjum and Ali Raza were my uncle's friends from Pakistan. They held our hands through many things, from teaching me to do halal grocery shopping to buying a car. They took us around the city and provided life advice as we drove around. They invited us to their house parties, the first of many *Desi* parties Bilal and I were to attend.

I filled up my days with talking on the phone, speaking to contacts from Pakistan. Chicago had a big South Asian diaspora and I also made a couple of Indian friends in my apartment building. The people I knew in Chicago all had families with children. I soon grew impatient with the conversations around what foods would make the best take away lunch for my husband, navigating post-holiday sales and the urgency to have children. My culture raised girls to be daughters, wives and mothers. Though most of my fellow female expatriates felt pride in supporting their spouses' career paths and aspirations, I had started to find this notion in conflict with my own identity. The negativity of emotions finally caught up with me. I craved to see my family but could not visit them. A trip back home would have meant going again to the US embassy in Pakistan for my return, which was notorious for refusing visa applications and denying entry into the United States. During that first year in Chicago, there were times when I was ready to call off my marriage, quit it all and go back to my family. My husband was distraught and totally clueless as to how he should address this.

Bilal and I had an arranged marriage. We were engaged for a year and a half before our marriage, which gave us some time to get to know each other, but our conversations were limited to those in artificial and congenial settings, at upscale coffee shops, dinner outings or surrounded by many people at family gatherings. As others of our generation in Pakistan, before marriage, we had always lived at our parents' homes who had provided not only for our professional and graduate education, but also living expenses while we lived with them. We had no idea how to run a house. Here in the American Midwest, not only did we have to figure out life, but also each other. It was not easy. We realized that we both had a temper. We both had strong ties to our families, which sometimes made it hard to provide space for another's family. I wanted from Bilal a promise to return to Pakistan once he finished residency, while he was becoming more resolute to spend the rest of our lives in America with every passing day. Though most South Asian women found their calling in homemaking, I found this role claustrophobic. Chicago's perpetually cold weather did not help either. I felt as if I was fighting many battles and losing them all.

For reasons unknown even to myself, I never spoke to my family about what I was going through. I was close not only to my parents but to many of my aunts and uncles, in whom I had confided several times while growing up. But, at this traumatic and lonely juncture in my life, all that my family back home heard was about the perfect bliss my marriage had turned out to be. My visa restrictions did not allow me to visit Pakistan and it would be a few years before I would be reunited with them. They all, however, were happy for my exciting life in the United States.

As I look back, this was also something I had unconsciously adopted from my culture. Talking about mental health was a taboo and I had never seen anyone open up and share personal problems and emotions. Raised to perfection, a Pakistani daughter's duty was to make her family proud. To "accommodate" in one's marital life was an essential characteristic of a good daughter. It was therefore not surprising that many Pakistani women in the West, became depressed at a later age, after spending years on the same trajectory where I was headed.

As I started spiraling out, Bilal, in his anxiety, sought help in an unlikely but only person he could confide in. This was Aftab *bhai*.

Aftab *bhai* was Bilal's acquaintance from Pakistan. They had grown up in the same neighborhood and he was one of my brother-in-law's good friends. Married and divorced at a young age during a turbulent time of his life, Aftab *bhai* understood the sensitivity of a marriage. He became my counselor and confidante. At a time when I did not drive, he helped with the groceries, offered money to attend a college and encouraged me to get any job that came my way. I finally secured work in the specialty jewelry department at a prestigious retail giant, Marshall Fields, at their flagship store on Chicago's State Street.

The retail position at Marshall Fields was not my dream job. A career in sales was no less than a nightmare and I was warned about it before moving to the United States. "Pakistanis only drive cabs, work at gas stations or stores in America," many people had warned me. My parents back home did not find pride in the fact that I was now working a jewelry counter, even if it was at a prestigious retailer. It was only a store after all!

But Marshall Fields did for me what no human being could do. It put me on a bullet train of Americanization. I sold expensive merchandise and made friends. I met Jesus (pronounced as Hae-sus),

17

my first Latinx and openly gay acquaintance. We became good friends and one day he dared me to try sushi. I had my first taste of raw fish and did not like it at all. I discovered Potbelly's sandwich shop across from Marshall Fields. To this day, I would pass on any other food for a Potbelly's sandwich.

Working at Marshall Fields brought me happiness and that joy was reflected in my life. After six months of staying in the Medical District, Bilal and I decided to change residences and rent a one-bedroom apartment on Sheridan Road, by North Lake Shore Drive. We both loved the beach and spent long hours on the shore of Lake Michigan, which was now in our backyard. As Bilal finished his first year of internship, his schedule relaxed. We spent more time together, sometimes meeting downtown after work and going for a movie and dinner.

We developed a small circle of Pakistani friends we had met mostly through Bilal's work at Sinai Children's Hospital. We hosted each other at homes and cooked tons of food. Sometimes, we would get together at Sabri Nihari or Usmania restaurant on Devon Street, popularly known as the "Dewaan" among Chicago's *Desi* community.

The *Desi* in America are a fascinating phenomenon. The word *Desi* is derived from the word des in Persian and desa in Sanskrit, which means land or country. In Pakistan, *Desi* is used as a slur synonymous to hillbilly. On the contrary, in the United States, *Desi* is a loaded term. On the surface, it signifies South Asian ethnicity, but inhabits hidden layers of meaning within itself. Racially, *Desis* are people defined by their brown skin and hail from the Indian subcontinent, which primarily includes India, Pakistan, Bangladesh and other countries in the South Asian region.

There are both external and internal nuances to be a *Desi*. To other ethnic communities, *Desis* are a model minority. From Pakistani doctors and engineers to Indian IT professionals, *Desis* have one aim in mind, that is, their American experiment cannot fail. They live in suburban homes, situated in the best school districts. Men work long hours covering holidays that no one else wants to work and the lives of women revolve around children and home. Our food requires extensive cooking, simmering flavors and lots of good Yankee candles to get those aromas out of our weather-proof homes in the United States. *Desi* women spend mornings in the kitchen before it is time for kids to return from school. They drive their kids to after-school math enrichment, sports lessons, dance classes and religio-cultural schools over the weekend.

Internally, within the community, the *Desis* pride themselves on their prudence. We love to haggle, and unconsciously equate every dollar that we spent to our home currency. A good *Desi* never spends on immaterial objects. The spiritual notion of "experience" never quite gels with us. A majority of us drive Japanese cars and the more affluent like German gas- guzzlers. We drill the *Desi* ethic of hard work and mistrust of everything non-*Desi* in our children. The second generation of *Desis*, coming of age in the United States, is therefore aptly called "ABCD," that stands for, "American Born Confused Desi."

Desis relax over the weekend at *Desi* parties. Since Islam prohibits consumption of alcohol, the Muslim section of the *Desi* population has found a replacement in *chai*, a South Asian way of preparing tea with plenty of milk and sugar. Every weekend, we like to get together over elaborate meals of *biryani*, *kebabs* and goat curry, followed by long sessions of *chai*, late into the night.

During those early days in Chicago, becoming an American *Desi* was an integral part of my immigration experience. I was inducted into the *Desi* community in Chicago, but it was not until the later years in Pittsburgh that I was completely immersed in the experience. Becoming an American *Desi* meant we were all working towards concrete material goals. We had to make money, have two cars with one of them preferably a luxury SUV to show up in at *desi* parties, save enough money before we have children to buy a suburban home in the best school district or to be able to send them to a private school. The newbies, especially those on non-immigrant visas like Bilal and myself, also had to accumulate resources to fund multiple visa and status transfers over the years, leading up to US citizenship.

The life of the immigrant community in the United States revolves around one singular goal, that is, how to make our stay in this country permanent. My generation of immigrants was more resolute about it than any other before us. America was not an El Dorado, but still provided refuge from unemployment and sectarian violence that many immigrants were grateful to have escaped in their native countries. The American immigration process is a money pit for those like Bilal and me, who required multiple visa and status transfers on our way to citizenship. People borrowed their way into becoming an American and found themselves in heavy debts by the time the process is complete. A fee hike of ten percent in application and procedural fees was expected every two to three years.

The material values I was self-learning in America were very different from my puritanical upbringing in a middle-income household in a developing country. My father, Wasim Adil, or Abu as I call him, was a professor of physics and a lifelong teacher. My mother, Rubab, Ami to me, had forsaken her career in banking after the birth of my brother, her second child. She worked for some time as a schoolteacher but then also let that go in the interest of raising children. Together, they provided us, their three children, a life that was safe, secure and joyous. There was enough of everything, but it was not abundant.

Another formative influence on my life were my three grandparents. My paternal grandparents, Abbajan and Mummy were another set of parents for me. One of the earliest gifts I remember receiving from Abbajan was a large picture book, Heidi, when I was four. I remember going to a bookstore with Abbajan and picking up the book. As I grew older, this evolved into a yearly trip during summer break, to the local book market in Karachi, known as the Urdu Bazaar.

My maternal grandmother, Nani Ami to her eighteen grandchildren, was a force to reckon with. A strong, independent woman from times when it was not considered an asset for a woman to be strong or independent-minded, Nani Ami was widowed at an early age, with six children. Resilience and willfulness became part of her nature, as she worked and saw her children through education and marriages. My husband would often remark that I had acquired my stubborn gene from her. Nani Ami's life had demanded prudence and she was thrifty and cautious in the use of all things including the carpet in her family room, on which all must tread carefully.

But, in a far-off land, away from my family, retail therapy brought me comfort. A lethal mix of American consumerism that I experienced at Marshall Fields combined with the *Desi* obsession of acquiring the best at the cheapest cost, took over my life for the next few years. I would become a deal maniac for branded merchandise, hoarding off-season stuff from clearance racks to use during the next season. I would also share news of sales with other desi friends so they could grab the deals in time. Sometimes, they would descend from their suburbs to Marshall Fields in Downtown to shop on my employee discount.

One April morning, as I climbed up the stairs of the State Street subway station for work at Marshall Fields, I found myself gasping for breath. I felt burned out and sick. It turned out that I was pregnant. Bilal and I were expecting our first child. The first doctor's visit revealed that I was already three months into pregnancy.

As a new life grew inside me, it was time for fresh beginnings. Bilal was offered a fellowship position in the Pediatrics Neurology Division at the University of Pittsburgh Medical Center (UPMC) Children's Hospital of Pittsburgh, in Pennsylvania. We decided to move, despite inhibitions that came with relocating yourself to what looked like an all-white-town in Appalachia.

Little did I know that one day, this small town would hold a piece of my heart like no other place ever had. Pittsburgh would become home.

. 2 .

YINZER TOWN

"In a way, I was born twice. I was born in 1934 and again in 1955 when I came to Pittsburgh. I am thankful to say that I lived two lives."

-Roberto Clemente, baseball legend, Pittsburgh Pirates

The first time I heard the name of an American city called Pittsburgh, my fate was already sealed with it. My husband had preemptively decided that if all went well with the interview at the UPMC Children's Hospital of Pittsburgh, that would be his place of choice among several other fellowship positions he had already nailed. Well it went, and we were off to Pittsburgh. Before we left Chicago, I had already extracted a promise from him to return to the city once he completed his training in four years.

My courtship period with the Steel City was a rocky one. We moved in November 2005, when I was five months pregnant with Sabina. While looking for housing, we would keep on getting lost across Pittsburgh's network of winding roads and tunnels. We could not tell where the Blue Belt ended and the Green started, which turned out to be a common way in which Pittsburghers explained addresses. The mountains and tunnels made me nauseous and the gray skies of October looked uninviting.

It did not help that the sprawling metropolis of Karachi and Chicago were my idea of cities. Chicago, with all its Hollywood luster, had meant America for me. Pittsburgh's narrow streets and lack of diversity scared me. In 2005, the city was still recovering from financial hardship it had declared the prior year, and signs of distress were visible on its roads and pavements. UPMC Children's Hospital was located in the neighborhood of Oakland at that time. We would have preferred to stay in that area but failed to find reliable and safe housing in Oakland. We ended up in the neighborhood of Greentree. Friends, who introduced us to Greentree's Crane Village Apartments, commended it as an affordable housing closer to the city with ample free parking to host *Desi* parties.

Pittsburgh was different from Chicago. There was no one on the streets of Pittsburgh who looked or talked like me. There was no Devon there. Our residence in Greentree isolated us from the rest of the Pakistani community, which primarily resided in the Eastern and Northern suburbs of the city. Muslim Community Center of Greater Pittsburgh (MCCGP) had emerged as a hub for *Desi* Muslims in contrast to the Islamic Center of Pittsburgh (ICP) which catered mostly to Muslim students at the University of Pittsburgh and people from the Middle East. A part of MCCGP's community would later form the Muslim Association of Greater Pittsburgh (MAP) for the convenience of Muslims residing in the Northern suburbs of Pittsburgh.

Pittsburgh was a city divided by geography. Topography determined demographics. The affluent lived on the Hills, in the North and the South, which both had some of the best schools in the region. There were also Polish Hill, the predominantly Black Hill District and the majorly Jewish Squirrel Hill. The neighborhoods existed on different sides of mountains and rivers, physically distancing the locals. At one point in history, this geographical disconnect between different parts of Pittsburgh had played an important role in keeping the city segregated. This fact was often mentioned in later years, when Pittsburgh would confront the brutal mistakes of its past in the shocking death of Antwon Rose, a seventeen- year- old Black teenager, and later during the Tree of Life massacre in the same year.

Pittsburgh's modern urban developers had tried to improvise on the geographical disconnect through a network of tunnels and bridges. However, a desire to artificially integrate different neighborhoods, could not bridge the racial and class divide this city had experienced from its earlier days as a blue-collar town. During the early twentieth century, Italian and Polish immigrants had provided working hands for the steel mills but did not find a place on Pittsburgh's millionaire row with the Fricks and the Carnegies. Today, the highways and a non-existent public transportation system have created a natural disconnect, between those who can afford to have a car per family member in a household and those who cannot afford such a luxury.

During those early months in Pittsburgh, I felt like an uprooted tree in a city where people prided themselves on their "Yinzer" genealogy. I was a "transplant," a nomenclature even those who had lived in Pittsburgh for twenty years went by. In the Steeler Nation, Pittsburghese was the official language. Football was the religion. During my second month in Pittsburgh, while traveling in a cab, the driver looked at me in disbelief when I failed to show any excitement as the Steelers quarterback, Ben Roethlisberger, known to Pittsburghers as "Big Ben" passed by on his motorcycle, right by our cab. Today, I can imagine the horror that the poor driver must have had at my apathy.

On March 18, 2006, after four months in Pittsburgh, Sabina came into our lives. I started exploring Pittsburgh with my new baby. Our fondest memories of the time were built at the Children's Museum and Greentree Public Library. I read "The Great Gatsby" and reread "To Kill a Mockingbird" which I had read in the past but could now better appreciate having been exposed to racial disparities in America. Our regular presence at the library's morning story time inducted Sabina fast into the Mother Goose culture. Through the likes of Yankee Doodle and Bill Grogan's Goat, I further caught up on the American slang.

We found a few like-minded friends with young children of their own. Bilal became an unofficial pediatrician for colic and ear infections, a go-to concierge physician for our ever-growing circle of friends and their babies. One of my neighborhood friends from India, Alvira and I, would frequent the Children's Museum of Pittsburgh along with our two baby girls, who turned into toddlers in an instant. During the warmer temperatures, we would plan picnics at Pittsburgh's many parks or outdoor spaces, complete with *biryani* and *chai*. Moraine State Park was an all-time favorite, with Settlers Cabin Park and Raccoon Creek State Park as close seconds.

Pittsburgh spring was the best. It was during my first spring in Pittsburgh, in April 2006, that I realized the reason why spring was considered the harbinger of life. As an English major, during my college days in Pakistan, I had curiously delved into British poetry, always wondering what it was like to see the first blooms. As the brown tree barks turned green with the first buds, snow melted, and birds changed colors with the scenery, I could not help but marvel at the picturesque developments I saw from my patio door at the Crane Village Apartments.

It was also during my first few months with a new baby and limited social time that I became addicted to and binge-watched every single season of the American soap opera, Desperate Housewives. My viewing time, however, was not restricted to TV. I started seeing these characters all around myself. I was surrounded not only by Karens, but also by *Desi* versions of the ladies from Wisteria Lane. These women tried to keep themselves amused while their husbands worked long hours. And I promised myself, never to become a caricature of American housewifeliness.

The sad truth was, that I sometimes did feel like one, hanging out with the affluent Pakistani community of Pittsburgh. The former steel town was trying to rebrand itself as the city of Eds & Meds and Tech. There was a disproportionately large Pakistani physician community in Pittsburgh, employed by the various hospitals as well as private practices. Their wives, some of whom I called good friends, reminded me of Bree Van de Camp, keeping up the semblance of a perfect relationship while silently embattling internal family crises created by busy husbands, an abundance of money and teenage children who grew increasingly distant from their Pakistani parents as they grew up. Many of these women were immigrants like me and missed family and home. We had playdates for children in their immaculately maintained houses with manicured yards and personal playgrounds costing thousands of dollars. While the children played, we hung around Ethan Allen dining tables with pastries and *samosas*. These ladies had designer personas and could pass as advertisements for Coach and Gucci, top down.

There were parties to plan and always more to attend. There was bonding, gossip and an abundance of social politics. If you were not at the table, you were on the table. Women talked about clothes, handbags and jewelry. Men talked about cars, politics and the best money exchange to send dollars back home to parents and family. Some common topics of interest included airline ticket prices from America to Pakistan and the best times to visit our native land. The best, in case of visits to the homeland, was defined both economically and seasonally, according to the heat index of the city one was going to visit with their "American" children.

These Pakistanis who now called themselves Americans, had come from different parts of Pakistan. Many hailed from small towns and cities and were the first of their families to attend college and professional school. While some proudly shared their rags to riches stories at the *Desi* parties, some others tried to hide them behind special edition Hummers and BMWs. And we all had lots of *chai*.

By the time my husband completed his fellowship training in 2009, we were expecting our second daughter. He was offered a job at the UPMC Children's Hospital and it looked like a good idea to stay rather than move in the middle of another pregnancy. Our family was blossoming and needed a bigger place to grow. Alina was born in November 2009 and right after, we moved to a townhouse in Wexford in the Northern suburbs of Pittsburgh. With the promise of a six-figure salary, two beautiful children and a suburban home, our American dream was finally complete.

The responsibilities of two children, coupled with homeownership and without much support tied me to the family and the house. There was not much else to do, except reveling in socializing, with two kids in tow. However, this period also provided an opportunity for soul-searching and reflection on where life was headed for me, at a personal level. From a vantage point, my life would look enviable and perfect. But there was a voice inside me that demanded more from life. I was still the girl who dreamed of being recognized for herself, for her strength of character and personality. I desired to preserve that younger me inside myself and not start living my life through the achievements of my husband and children.

The problem was, I did not know where to start. I was full of doubt. I had many questions about my existence to which I had no answers. Was I ready to let go my personal dreams and ambitions for our family unit? Did I want to spend the rest of my life bearing children and staying home? Was my calling in life to be a wife and a mother or was there another or more importantly better purpose to it? With two young kids and most of my immigrant girlfriends trapped in the same situation as myself, there was no way to look for inspiration or advice.

What I was experiencing at that time is an existentialist dilemma many immigrants in America go through at some point in their life. We live in constant fear of our children "going bad" which might mean many things from cultural attrition to loss of religio-cultural practices. Its extreme form is the nightmare a family might have to face if one of their children married a person outside of their culture.

In the *Desi* section of the American Muslim culture, the children's "going bad" is directly correlated to a mother's career aspirations. "Her daughter married a *gora* because the child had spent her entire childhood in a daycare. See, this is what happens when you don't give time to your children when they are young. If you leave your children with these Americans, obviously they will learn to be like them." Such statements were often made by the gossip mongers not only at weddings of mixed ethnicity but also days before and after it. The idea, of course, is not research-based, but many times served as a self-fulfilling prophecy to the amusement of our community. I desired to break free from the shackles of these ideas, as well as people who perpetuated them, but found myself at a loss when it was time for action. I was caught in a vicious circle.

Then, in 2011, Bilal and I went for *Hajj*, a pilgrimage to Mecca in Saudi Arabia. All Muslims who have physical and financial means to undertake this journey are required to perform Hajj once in a lifetime. The pilgrimage provided a beautiful opportunity for us not only to spiritually bond but also reconnect in a way we had not been able to do for a long time amidst chaos of navigating parenthood and home ownership. I had always kept up with the Islamic rituals of praying five times a day and fasting, but it was only during *Hajj* that I felt spiritually connected to God. I prayed to *Allah* for providing me guidance and opportunity to find my calling, whatever that might be. I felt my life had no purpose, and asked Allah for a sign to define things for me.

The world looked beautiful from the patio of my home in the North Hills of Pittsburgh. But both local and international news made me feel guilty of sitting home and sighing while the wars raged in Iraq and Afghanistan. Children from West Africa to Pittsburgh were dying of hunger and violence. It was also during those years that I started to realize my privilege: the privilege of being an educated elite. I felt trapped in my bubble but desired to break out of the comfort zone.

The Graduate School of Public and International Affairs (GSPIA) at the University of Pittsburgh gave me the breakthrough that I needed. "I grew up in Pakistan in the 1980s when people talked about Russian–Afghan war on the streets. I had witnessed firsthand the plight of refugees as well as what it means for a country to provide refuge for others on its meager resources." This thesis was the premise of my graduate school essay, where I applied and was accepted in the Master of Public and International Affairs (MPIA) program, with a major in Human Security. I started coursework in Fall 2012.

Education at an American university opened doors for me in unique ways. It led to my Americanization in ways different than Marshall Fields. This was the world of jargon and buzzwords, of economics, discovering creative solutions to global inequities and affecting policies. Our classes were the hub for resolving world problems. However, somewhere along the way, while writing policy papers on the Syrian civil war, I became interested in finding local parallels.

Like any graduate school, GSPIA was full of young ambitious students. The majority of the student body was in its mid-twenties, partly driven by the lack of employment opportunities after college, during a recession. Right from the beginning, during the first semester, people started planning summer gigs in Washington DC and internships in Uganda and Somalia. I, meanwhile, at thirty-three years of age, with two children and a very busy husband, had to spend several hours making childcare and dinner arrangements before committing to a happy hour. Anything out of Pittsburgh was out of question for me. I had to find internships and build US credentials. I was supposed to attend networking events, make elevator pitches and small talk. I was brought up in a culture of humility. I was taught not to talk about myself. If I had "real merit" someone else should be talking about it as my reference. But now, I was required to market myself! I realized later that as nice and helpful as they were, I needed more than professional counseling that the student counselors at GSPIA could provide. I needed life-coaching.

I was raised to be a homemaker in Pakistan and not in America.

In my home country, if I had decided to spend time outside of home, to go to school or work, I would have the support of my family and in-laws in raising children. There would be household help to make dinners and a chauffeur to pick and drop children from school. My husband would have his own family and friends to hang out with until I would come home, and we would all happily sit down for dinner, have *chai* afterwards and go to bed. Next morning, we would take out our perfectly ironed clothes from closets and go on with our lives.

This was not how my life looked in the United States of America while I attended graduate school. The realities of my life only created chaos with our clothes in piles all over the house and all of us coming home tired and exhausted at the end of the day. We would eat out all the time and had little time to exercise. Einstein Bros. Bagels at William Posvar Hall and free pizza at GSPIA seminars became my lunch meals. There were no times to rest or play. By the end of the day, we were all tired and cranky. By the end of my grad school, my husband and I would have each put on twenty pounds.

I had to find a way of adulting through graduate school without isolating myself. I had to talk to people who have been in situations like mine who had juggled young families with professional responsibilities. Diane Roth Cohen, Assistant Director at Ford Institute for Human Security, became my friend and mentor at this time. With her no-nonsense attitude, Diane gently pushed me towards excellence and helped carve out a place for myself in the island of over-achievers that GSPIA was. She provided advice and support, always reminding me of the importance of networking, and taking time out to do it amidst a barrage of requirements for policy papers and deadline for presentations. Diane wrote letters of recommendation for me and finally connected me to an opportunity that made me a Yinzer for life.

In Fall 2013, Diane shared with me a coveted internship opportunity at Allegheny County's Department of Human Services (DHS), Immigrants and Internationals Initiative. The prestigious internship was not only a great opportunity to learn how the local government worked but also provided a stipend. But these, according to Diane, were not the only reasons why I should apply for the position.

Barbara Murock, known to all as Barb, was a great mentor and one of the pioneers of Diversity and Inclusion initiatives at Allegheny County. Barb served as the Manager for Immigrants and Internationals Initiative at DHS. With her simple yet eclectic tastes, meticulousness and passion for biking, Barb was the queen of her own universe. Born and raised in Pittsburgh, Barb was everyone's friend- from her neighbor, the County Executive to the Bhutanese and Somali refugees with whom she worked tirelessly on making public services more inclusive and accessible for all Pittsburghers. According to Diane, the internship would be a great opportunity to learn from and work with Barb. News went around that Barb knew everyone one should know to get things done in Pittsburgh.

I wrote to Barb and soon met with her for an interview. In less than a week, Barb asked me to join the Immigrants and Internationals Initiative, then, a small part of Allegheny County Department of Human Services. I was recruited to work on the new Refugees Seniors Engagement Committee in addition to the initiative's flagship Cultural Competency Committee. A traveler and free spirit, Barb held inclusion at the core of her mission. She embraced the concept of a global village, the way I had rarely seen anyone else do, especially the white baby boomers like her.

Working with Barb was great. Her attention to detail was unnerving. Not an email could leave any intern's desk without passing through Barb's watchful gaze. All interns would joke about our "Barbafied" emails which all would read the same no matter who among us had written them. Barb was an amazing editor and teacher. To this day, I never send out an email without highlighting important details in yellow and putting date and time in the email subject. The impacts of Barb's teaching have been everlasting.

Barb had created the Immigrants and Internationals Initiative (I&II) out of nothing. For the first few years, she single-handedly ran I & II with the help of graduate interns whom she liked hiring at least for a year at a time. Her passion for public service was contagious and trickled down to everyone she worked with. Under Barb's tutelage, I started going to places I had never visited before. South Hills Interfaith Ministry (SHIM), now called Prospect Park Family Center, located in the Baldwin-Whitehall area of Pittsburgh, was my first stop. I helped serve their vast Bhutanese clientele in the food pantry.

Gradually, as I realized my privilege, my illusions about being an immigrant in America started peeling off. I had only known one kind of immigrant, and those were people in my bubble, who were exactly like myself. There were many others who were not living the American dream but were happy to have escaped the nightmare. These refugees, who came from Bhutan, Iraq, Somalia, Burma and several other countries not too far from where I was born, had fled war and poverty. Some had spent years in refugee camps and were astonished at the abundance that sometimes even food pantries in America could afford to provide. Like me, they were flabbergasted by the choice of cereals available. Many also fast contracted ailments like diabetes and cardiovascular illnesses by consumption of starch rich diet their bodies were unaccustomed to.

I found working with refugees not only fulfilling but also introspective. Many Bhutanese refugees spoke Hindi, which was similar to my native Urdu. I could talk to some senior Bhutanese community members in Hindi, which they found comforting. I shared my Muslim roots with refugees from Iraq and Syria and we often talked about raising children in an increasingly Islamophobic America. We all worried about our family dinner in different ways. For me, it was a matter of contemplating the kind of meat to cook that night, while for many of my new refugee friends, it could mean a night at the soup kitchen.

There were gunshots in Pittsburgh. Every time there was a shooting my phone rang. I noticed that all phones around me would ring at the same time. Under Allegheny County's official protocol, all employees would receive a phone call in case of emergency, across the county. Sometimes, the shooting would be in Wilkinsburg or East Liberty. Most of the time, it would be in Mt. Oliver. I realized that before my work with the County, I had never visited these predominantly Black neighborhoods. Drug and gun cultures were rampant in these areas of the city due to lack of resources, little support for single parents and resource-constrained school districts. Though I had limited interaction with the Black community in Pittsburgh prior to 2014, after almost ten years of living in Pittsburgh, I dedicated my Capstone Research class on "Poverty, Inequality and Development" at GSPIA to *"Reducing African American Poverty in Pittsburgh Metropolitan Area Through Economic and Political Empowerment."*

Ironically, my awareness of systemic inequalities in Allegheny County grew during the year Pittsburgh had claimed to be the "most livable city in America." While the ratings touted the former steel town's renaissance reflected in gentrification of underserved areas, a revamped cultural district and the then new and evolving presence of the technology giant Google, there was another reality existing alongside. Poverty and crime existed in clusters hidden beneath the luster of the new and upcoming Pittsburgh.

It was during my brief time at Immigrants and Internationals Initiative that I found my calling for community service. It was there I met non-profit managers, local government officials and refugee leaders from across the region. Everyone said the same thing, that Pittsburgh had silos. We all worked hard to find the magic solution to tear down the walls and build resource connections. We worked on providing cultural competency training for organizations that served Pittsburgh's diverse and immigrant communities. We advocated and empowered the least resourceful among us, which was empowering for all of us in a unique way.

One unique opportunity presented itself in the summer 2014. From thousands of candidates around the country, I was selected to be a finalist for a Presidential Appointee position with the Obama Administration. I interviewed at the White House, for a role at The U.S. Department of Health and Human Services (HHS). Though I did not find it in me to relocate from Pittsburgh at that time, for academic and personal reasons, the selection itself affirmed my faith in my adopted homeland, where merit was the key. An immigrant like me, without any connections in higher offices, had a fair share at opportunity and resources, equivalent to those who have been here before me. Those two days of interview at the White House were an experience in themselves, providing a rare insight into a world, which looked fascinating and scary at the same time.

To keep up with my part-time work for the County, I had gone part-time at grad school. These two part-time jobs made it full-time. The grad school was academically demanding and my work at I&II, though professionally fulfilling, not only commanded time but could also be emotionally exhausting. I was working as one of the smallest pegs of a big bureaucracy. The work was meaningful, but change was slow. I barely had any time to spend with my family. While my husband had found a new passion in playing squash, our girls spent most of their time at home with babysitters, who by that time had become our family's lifelines.

I was reminded everyday by people around me that I was failing in my duty as a Muslim mother. One of the biggest immigrant concerns is loss of native culture in a foreign land. For Muslim immigrants, it is accompanied by a fear of moral decay signified most outwardly by alcohol consumption and dating. Just like the West would judge Eastern cultures for arranged marriages, overbearing parents and Muslim women for covering their heads, we are wary of the Westerners for the absurdity of letting their children find their life partners through trial and error, letting them move out at eighteen and women in shorts. Muslim immigrant parents would indeed disown their daughter before other fellows Muslims see her in "short shorts." A good Muslim mother stayed home and watched over children so they could be saved from any disgrace that the Western society could prompt them to do. Even letting kids, especially girls, leave home to attend college was a big taboo, forcing many girls to attend community and local colleges instead of a school of their choice. The rules were laid not by Islamic jurisprudence but by the conservative and patriarchal cultures of Muslim countries.

At social gatherings, the "moral police" never failed to remind me that the babysitters would expose my girls to what I was supposed to protect them from. Who knew, anyways, what those babysitters were up to? If they were young, they probably had boyfriends, who were likely visiting my place while I was not there. If they were old, they might be abusive. At the least, they all probably smoked and got drunk. And then the ultimate fear; they wore "short shorts" and would inundate my pure Muslim girls into the same culture. Our little Alina, who had spent most of her four years of life between daycare and babysitters, did not speak Urdu. Sabina was fast forgetting it, too. The fact that they both were more organized and followed schedules to the minute, which was something I, like most of my fellow *Desi* homemaker friends, could never establish, was conveniently overlooked for the greater good of raising good Muslims who spoke Urdu.

But my greater crime at that time was more personal. I was busy but happy. However, I did not have the time to make those around me happy. As *Desi* dinners, *kitty parties* and extensive socializing continued around me, I had to purposefully distance our family from it. Many of my community members and friends interpreted this as snobbery on my part. We had no time to host lavish dinners and people stopped inviting us. I was made aware every day how my kids were growing up without religion and culture, just because we were not mingling with the *Desi* crowd on a daily basis.

By the last semester of graduate school, I was physically and emotionally exhausted. I started developing a variety of illnesses from allergies to untended minor injuries that developed into sores. I had no time to see the doctor. I had to take some time off from everything I was doing to go through a laser therapy treatment for my foot.

As I stopped for a couple of days, I wondered why I was running so much. I turned to my husband and he had no answers for me. He was only being supportive of what looked like my passion. I was at the crossroads where I had to let my body heal and needed some room to breathe.

With two months short of completing a year, I let my work at Allegheny County go. I had reserved the toughest classes at GSPIA, including a Capstone seminar, for my last semester. I refocused on completing school, which I did finally, in December 2014.

Barb, meanwhile, nominated me to serve on the Advisory Board of Immigrants and Internationals Advisory Council, to be a representative of the Muslim Community of Pittsburgh. It helped me maintain a network of like-minded enthusiasts, people I could count on to fill service gaps, whenever needed.

My life took an important step as Bilal and I became naturalized citizens of the United States of America in February 2015. It turned out to be the coldest day of the year, and Sabina ended up accompanying us to the Naturalization Ceremony because of snow day at school. Barb and her team were there to congratulate and support us, as Bilal and I shared our story of "making it in America" with the audience. We were now proud Americans, who could participate in the civic and political life of the country. With the presidential election coming up in 2016, that meant the world to me.

Though immigrants through the ages, with or without statuses on a piece of paper, have written their stories with sweat and blood, in the larger American narrative, becoming a US citizen is a rite of passage to achieve legitimacy in this country. In some ways, it is a test of one's resilience. My own naturalization as an American citizen imbibed me with a spirit to be part of the civic and political process of the country that was now my own. If GSPIA had turned me into a global thinker, I&II encouraged me to be a local actor. I had always enjoyed writing, but I started picking up the pen more regularly. My issues were local, born and bred in Pittsburgh. Pittsburgh became the microcosm of my universe and I was infused with a desire to be a part of the legacy of this city.

Somewhere along the way, I also became a *Muslimah*.

. 3 .

AMERICAN MUSLIMS

"If you are an American Muslim, you live in a community that is really struggling to get its feet off the ground. We are a very young community so to speak, institutionally and otherwise. The way in which we are portrayed it's like we are the empire from Star Wars and the truth is that we'd be lucky to be the rebel alliance."

-Haroon Moghul, Muslim author and activist

American Muslims, like American *Desis*, are an "American phenomena." Nowhere else in the world would you find Muslims like them. Like many other roles I had to partake after migrating to the United States, I now had to be baptized as an American *Muslimah*.

To be a *Muslimah,* and that too an American one, was an overbearing concept for someone like me. It meant not only to learn how to be one myself, but also how to raise my two girls to have a sense of belonging for this up and coming demographic in the American landscape. My experience of growing up, as part of the *Sunni* Muslim majority in a predominantly Muslim country was very different to the life that I now had to live as a member of the Muslim minority in the United States.

Like America itself, American Muslims are a diverse group of people. Against popular belief that Muslims and Islam are new to America, historical records show that Muslims accompanied Christopher Columbus on the voyage that led to the discovery of America. Muslims were part of many European expeditions of antiquity as mapmakers and guides. The Muslim Renaissance, which spanned over several hundred years from the eight to fifteenth century, produced historians, mathematicians, explorers and oceanographers who perfected the art and science of cartography through exact measurements and vividly descriptive travelogues. The Muslim presence in Spain, helped resource sharing of intellect and ideas across Europe, that eventually led to the discovery of the New World in the Americas.

However, most indigenous American Muslims trace their lineage to the African continent, from where they were brought on ships as slaves via the transatlantic slave trade during the sixteenth to nineteenth century. Many Muslim slaves continued to practice their religion, mostly under hardship but sometimes also under owners who allowed religious freedom. Indeed, an important aspect of the civil rights movement in America was the revival of the Islamic faith as its very American brand Nation of Islam, founded by Wallace D. Fard Muhammad in 1930. The Nation was initially embraced by American leaders like Malcolm X and Muhammad Ali. Unlike Sunnis, Shias and many other sects of Islam, which originated in the Eastern parts of the world, The Nation of Islam and its followers were essentially a product of the United States of America.

The voluntary migration of Muslims from different parts of the world to the United States started during the 1920s. But it was the Immigration and Naturalization Act of 1965 that abolished the previous quota-based immigration for countries and established a new system of immigration based on family reunification and skilled labor. After the passage of the Act, Muslims came from Turkey, Middle East and South Asia seeking refuge and economic opportunity in El Dorado, like people from many other nations. The desire to migrate to America was intensified by the fantasies created in the minds of aspiring immigrants, which perpetuated images of the American streets as if they were "paved with gold."

The American Muslims in 2020, a cluster that I belong to, is comprised of approximately 58 percent of first generation immigrants, 18 percent of those with immigrant parents, and another 24 percent who are described as third generation or those born to American parents. Together we comprise a little less than 1 percent of the total American population.

Small numbers and an aura of "otherness" have shaped generations of American Muslim experience. A vast majority of American Muslim families have been practicing social distancing, from other communities, since times unknown. We are not fond of pets, especially dogs, given the popular belief that the presence of dogs keeps good angels away from one's house. There is no rhyme or reason as to how this cultural myth would have originated, but it has definitely played a role in keeping us away from dogs and social networking, while Americans are bonding over their favorite topic, that is, talking about their dogs. In a country where people treat their pets as children, our pet of choice is often a fish. We find ourselves left out of conversations and small talk at workplace gatherings and parties, not only because of our aversion to man's best friend but also because of dietary restrictions. Not only do we not consume wine or pork, we exist in constant terror of consuming it by mistake. Many Muslims, especially of South Asian descent only consume meat slaughtered according to the *halal* certification, which mandates that the meat is from butcheries that are certified according to Muslim religious guidelines. The practice is similar to the observance of kosher guidelines in the Jewish community.

The act of slaughtering animals according to Islamic guidelines is called *zabiha* and internally, within the community, American Muslims are unofficially categorized as *zabiha* or *non-zabiha* people.

Just like the rest of America judges Muslims for their unconventional dietary and social habits, the *zabiha* and *non-zabiha* guys are always at loggerheads with each other. The validity of the claim that Muslims could only consume *zabiha halal* meat had prompted many post-party fierce debates and aggressive arguments. At the end of it, we had all been beneficiaries of the *zabiha halal* specialty restaurants, which had enriched the American landscape with their amazing kebabs and lamb stews.

Hijab is another categorization, or rather bone of contention, that divides the American Muslim diaspora, especially Muslim women. The American Muslim women world is divided into *hijabis* and *non-hijabis*, unlike my native Pakistan, where I hardly knew any women among family and friends who wore hijab. In Pakistan, those who chose to cover their head did so for strictly religious reasons and it had no connotations of identity politics.

This is different in the United States, among American Muslim women.

The word hijab connotes with "cover" and "modesty" in Arabic and Eastern languages. In popular diction, *hijab* is a piece of cloth that Muslim women use to cover their head and sometimes face. As against common perception that Muslim women are forced into covering their head, for most American women, practicing *hijab* is a matter of choice. According to the Institute of Social Policy and Understanding (ISPU) out of more than 40 percent of American women of the Islamic faith who say they wear *hijab*, 54 percent do so either as an act of piety, 21percent to be identified as a Muslim and 12 percent for modesty. Only 1percent wear *hijab* because a family member requires it. The practice of observing *hijab* is, as such, very personal for the Muslim women in America compared to some parts of the world where cultural norms dictate it. Those who observe it here are its passionate advocates for reasons mentioned above. They have been "called" to observe *hijab* at some point in their life and do not hesitate in spreading their light around and converting *non-hijabis* to their side of the aisle.

American Muslims in some large communities across the United States, like those in Michigan and Chicago, also found themselves divided between the *masjid* crowd and APPNA crowd. APPNA refers to the Association of Physicians of Pakistani Descent of North America and is known for its ostentatious retreats with gala-like conferences, lavish bazaar and displays of wealth. It attracted Pakistan's finest in America, whom those outside of this social circle, often referred to as "People with big houses and even bigger egos." The wealthy APPNA community had made its impact on the United States with empowerment only big money could bring. They led political action, supported medical scholarship and helped local communities with free medical support, especially in underserved parts of America. It provided a platform for Pakistani physicians, mostly Muslims, to come together. The pictures from their events often featured women in sleeveless Pakistani kurtas, standing alongside their male friends, unlike pictures from mosque events where men and women stood at a distance, with covered heads and lowered gazes.

Like other religions, proselytizing or *tableegh* is an important component of Islam. However, in the country of my birth, it was reserved for a special group of people whom others ran away from. While growing up in Pakistan, I had known women who covered or not covered their heads, or people who practiced the so-called religious or non-religious behavior, but their intentions and reasons were mostly personal. Proselytizing, however, was an important aspect of American Islam. It was used to impress and convert not only people of other faiths, but also a change of hearts within our own community. Over the years, many of my Muslim friends, especially those who grew up in America, would pass on varying degrees of religious literature to me, so I could become more of a Muslim.

For me, an immigrant from the Islamic Republic of Pakistan, American Islam was a consuming brand. I was born and brought up surrounded by Islam in a way that I never had to think about the burden of being a Muslim. I dressed how I dressed and ate what I ate, not as a religious choice or pressure, but because that was the only way of life, I was accustomed to. I never had to carry my identity on head or had felt the need even to proclaim it. I was a Muslim, only by virtue of being born into this faith, just like another person who was born into Christianity or Judaism. It was novel to me that my faith, clothing and habits could be considered exotica and a topic worth exploration and conversation.

For these very reasons, I might have been born a Muslim in Pakistan but my transformation into a practicing Muslim took place in America. America turned me into a Muslim by curious glances, excessive curiosity, brutal criticism and over-analysis of my faith and people. Though Muslims were a hidden part of America for a long time, pre-9/11, it was only after 2001, that our "unique" practices and beliefs became part of the American conversations from mainstream media to dinner tables. I remember once being at a gathering a night before *Eid* in 2007, where a news channel was broadcasting a program on Muslim holidays. One of the guests remarked how the portrayal of Muslims on American media resembled programs on animals on National Geographic, where distant researchers and narrators talked about a creature's habitat, food, micro and macro aggressions and what it could mean for the rest of the world, human beings and ecosystem. Like animals, Muslims were the subject but not part of writing the narrative.

In the immediate post-9/11 America, there were only two groups writing the Muslim story. Those were the US Republican Government and terrorist organizations like Al-Qaeda and Islamic State of Iraq and Syria, a terrorist group commonly known as ISIS. Muslims living in American neighborhoods, who enriched America everyday with their toil and taxes, were either living in denial or teaching their children never to respond to another child who called them a terrorist at school. As a community, the pre-9/11 immigrant American Muslims had kept to themselves and focused more on the ritualistic practices of Islam. They had founded mosques, as places of worship and cultural centers and were happy to stay enclosed in them, protecting their children from outside influence and criticism. Apolitical to a fault, they did not know how or want to prepare their children for the onslaught that they had to face in schools and neighborhoods, following the Sept. 11 attacks. They hushed up the trauma that many Muslim American youth of the time had to internalize. The aftermath was a generation that grew up to be patriotic Americans to the core, normalizing every slur and hateful comment sent their way, as part of proving their loyalty to the motherland.

Immigrants of my generation, however, were different. I did not live in the United States when the terrorist attacks of Sept. 11 happened and therefore, the burden and shame that the entire American Muslim community was made to carry at that time had escaped me. I was vocal about sharing my identity, ideas and criticism of how Muslims were portrayed in America. I was also not a product of the American Islamic day and weekend schools, which in their efforts to cater to the diversity within the Muslim community, had decided to strip themselves clear of arts and culture and present religion within a rigid box with clear checkmarks for right and wrong. On the other hand, I was raised in the *Barelvi school of thought* within Islam, which was close to *Sufism* and mystic practices. As a South Asian, my cultural practices, language and sensitivities were closer to Hindus than Muslims from other parts of the world, including those who had spent lives in America.

My colleagues at the Harold Washington Public Library, and later at Marshall Fields, were fascinated to have a pure, right-out-of-oven Muslim among them. They had never met one, or at least not one who could not perceive the danger of declaring herself a Muslim. They were intrigued when I fasted during Ramadan and could not believe that someone could go without food and water all day long.

However, just as intrigued America was by me, so was I with it, especially its Muslims. Like the rest of America, I was introduced to them on television channels, denouncing terrorism, giving explanations of and for their faith to hostile interviewers. Islam does not suppress women and no, we do not endorse terrorism: I was tired of hearing Muslim scholars and activists proclaim on cable channels again and again, but apparently non-Muslim Americans were having a hard time getting convinced.

Once I started going to the mosque, I met these American Muslims in-person. As a *non-zabiha, non-hijabi* woman, I found myself at the bottom of the American Muslim hierarchy, right from the onset. For many, I was a person destined for hell and my sins were going to be reflected on my children. Many of my American Muslim friends did not hesitate in chastising me on those grounds; "Think what your children would do when their mother eats KFC. Where would this culture take them?" During those early days of my marriage and time in America, it was hard for me to fathom such thoughts and I could not forsake my chicken drumsticks from KFC in the hope that those would one day doom my children.

American Islam had evolved more as a somewhat rigid brand of identity for a minority group rather than the soft version of my ancestors in South Asia. In the spirit of Pan Islamism and absence of a religious culture to accompany the religion to thrive, American Muslims looked to the hardcore practices of the Kingdom of Saudi Arabia, a country defined by the extremist ideology of *Wahhabism*. The fear of losing religion in a foreign land paralyzed immigrant parents, who centered their lives on raising "good Muslims." Muslims in America had come to be defined as a people who not only did not consume pork and alcohol but also abstained from music and arts. The Islamic Sunday schools, in an effort to maintain the cultural practice of arranged marriage, steered kids away from any kind of intergender relationships which in turn backfired by raising young men and women who failed to look at each other as potential spouses. Sunday schools promoted a culture where Muslim girls and boys did not talk to each, unlike regular day schools. Eventually, it produced a generation where young Muslim men and women refrained from talking and making alliances with each other but comfortably did so with those of other faiths and cultures.

To American Muslims, their version of Islam was the best and the most original. They claimed it to be scripture-centric, derived directly from the Quran since there were no cultural practices to "taint" it. Many popular American scholars of Islam were converts from other religions, and they emphasized the importance of practicing Islam, especially distanced from the South and Central Asian influences, which placed as much importance on the creation as on the creator. Today, the most popular American Muslim scholars and leaders are the ones who were born and raised in the United States. The first significant generation to come of age in America that was born to immigrant Muslim parents were the millennials. Indeed, the version of Islam practiced by the millennial Muslims and generations after was shaped and influenced by puritan views of the American Muslim scholars. Many of them claimed it to be Islamic Modernism.

This group of religious scholars emerged as a force in the years much after 9/11. They were well- rooted in American diction as well as Islamic vocabulary and appealed especially to the Muslim youth growing up in America who found it easier to relate to their ideas and accent, then to their parents. They became even more popular with the rise of the internet and YouTube and were instrumental in writing a more positive Muslim narrative, recounting many important contributions Muslims had made throughout the history of America. They also allied themselves with the Black community, which according to the Pew Research Institute, constituted a fifth of all Muslims, but had failed to find its accord with Muslims from South Asia and the Middle East. This new breed of imams recognized social media as an important instructional tool and shared words of wisdom and religion on Twitter, Facebook and Instagram. American to the core, they challenged the notion of Islam as an "immigrant" religion. They created "The New Muslim Cool," American in spirit, with bearded young men in Saudi-style tunics and hijab-clad girls, who proclaimed and asked for nonjudgmental mosques. At the same time, these young men and women looked down upon the version of Islam and foreign accents of their immigrant predecessors and contemporaries. In 2019, the keynote address at the Muslim Association of Greater Pittsburgh's (MAP) youth-inspired fundraising dinner was titled "Not your parents' mosque", disregarding the contributions of many parents who had been instrumental in the foundation of that mosque. Because of their peculiar habits, these American Muslims had become caricatures for other Muslims around the world and were often looked upon with curiosity, especially in a country like Pakistan. People abroad in Muslim countries, found it hard to mesh the image of a *hijab* clad woman who used extensive Arabic vocabulary, but at the same time listened to Western hip-hop and would not mind sipping on *huqqa* with religious devotion.

As American Islam evolved as a culture and an independent sect, it needed its own jargon. Arabic vocabulary filled this space and became integral to the American Muslim discourse. It took me a while to recognize that the JAK greeting at the end of emails of many of my Muslim brethren is an abbreviation for the Arabic phrase, *Jazāk Allāhu Khayran* that can be literally translated to "May Allah reward your efforts." This is how American Muslims thanked each other, unlike Muslims in many other parts of the world, where people simply said, "Thank You" in English or had words in local vernacular like the Urdu word *shukriya*. More surprising for me was the adoption of Arabic greetings and vocabulary as the Islamic vocabulary. The practice had taken roots and even those who came from the non-Arab speaking countries, like Pakistan, Turkey and Iran, had happily adopted the practice. It was important to invoke the name of Allah in everything one did or said. While in my native Pakistan, only the clerics peppered their vocabulary with words like *Masha Allah, Insha Allah* and *Subhan Allah*, my American born Muslim friends would frequently use these words to confirm movie plans and compliment each other's shades of lipsticks. If I had found this use of Arabic vocabulary as the language of choice for American Muslim linguistics, interesting and amusing, the rest of America was spooked by it for sure. These along with *Jihad, Sharia, Allahu Akbar* and many other Arabic words could be easily considered "terrorist vocabulary," as American media often displayed images of Middle Eastern and South Asian men from unknown lands on television, committing atrocities in the name of Islam, while using similar language.

Just like American English, I had to learn the American Muslim vocabulary too. I learned that we were all *brothers and sisters* in faith and referred to each other as such. My *hijab*-less and sans Muslim vocabulary persona, needed a crash course in becoming an American Muslim. I was fascinated as well as dismayed by the emphasis that the American Muslim culture placed on external components and an outward show of the Muslim identity. I was determined to learn and carve out a place for myself in this diaspora, that at one point looked like the only way my family and I could survive in America. We had to forsake our national identity to be part of a cultural force, however feeble it was. My naturalization as an American citizen had not claimed my native passport, but the American mosques did. Still, I would be chastised at times for always talking about Pakistan, in conversations about Islam as I saw it practiced while growing up in a Muslim country.

The American mosques Islamized me in no time. They proved to be the best teachers and as a student I was fascinated by my school as well as the academics it had to offer. Never before had I seen an institution more representative of the American values of free speech yet in doubt of free speech.

Our Sunday mornings and afternoons were spent at the Muslim Community Center of Pittsburgh (MCCGP), once Sabina started attending the Sunday school there in 2010. It took us forty minutes each way to travel to the MCCGP, but it was important for us to have our child grow as part of her people. I learned some of my earliest Islamic vocabulary with Sabina. There was a great emphasis on proper pronunciation of Arabic, the right way to cover the head and use of Arabic diction to mark every action and emotion from sneezing to using the bathroom.

In a year's time, it all started coming together. I was slowly converting into an American Muslim who never failed to say *Yarhamkullah* whenever someone sneezed. It was, therefore, a proud moment for me when in 2018, I was selected to teach a class on "Muslims in the Neighborhoods" at the Osher Lifelong Learning Institute (OLLI) at the University of Pittsburgh. It finally completed my induction into the American Muslim lifestyle. As some would say, I eventually became a "professional Muslim."

. 4 .

RAISING AMERICANS

"Do not raise your children the way (your) parents raised you, they were born for a different time."

-Ali Ibn Abi Thalib (RA), companion of Prophet Muhammad
(PBUH)

I was not born an American, but my children were. Like many other things in my life, I had no idea what to do with these tiny human beings whose life and welfare were entrusted to me. All I knew was that just like water in a vessel, the cradle of their experiences will shape them.

Our first daughter came into our lives after almost three years of marriage and within four months of moving to Pittsburgh. Like all first-time parents, Bilal and I were super excited and over-prepared. We had envisioned an organic and pristine existence for our firstborn. We took Lamaze classes and I decided to stay away from epidural at birth. I had indeed no idea what delivering a baby felt like and called for the medicine the moment my labor started. A baby girl came into our world on March 18, 2006. Following the Muslim tradition of giving a meaningful name to child, we decided to call her Sabina, which meant flower, in Arabic.

My mother had come all the way from Pakistan to help us with our firstborn. She had brought many gifts, which included *shalwar kameez* suits for me in larger sizes, kurtas for her son-in-law and many sweaters and warm clothing for the baby. She had also brought honey, which according to the tradition in Pakistan, is given to a newborn right after birth. It is claimed to be a *sunnah*, derived directly from the traditions practiced or advised by the Prophet Muhammad (PBUH). My mom was disappointed to hear about our concerns of botulism and modern-day advice against giving honey to babies before they turn one.

Sabina was diagnosed with jaundice due to a slightly high level of bilirubin at the time of birth. Before we left the hospital, the pediatrician had recommended natural phototherapy by spending a few hours each day in sunlight. The month of March in that cold Pittsburgh spring did not offer much in the way of warmth and sunlight. By the fifth day of her life, Sabina looked visibly pale and sick. We took her to UPMC Children's Hospital. Lab tests revealed a significantly higher bilirubin than previous testing. She was admitted to the intensive care unit and placed under infrared lights for phototherapy while physicians around us waited and watched if a blood transfusion would be required.

That day, I felt extremely helpless. Tears streamed down my eyes at the sight of needles in my baby's tiny arms and limbs. My Sabina, my little peanut, was battling for life in an incubator. We could only wait and pray for a miracle. And a miracle did happen. Sabina responded fast to therapy and left the intensive care in a few hours.

We spent the next five days at the Children's Hospital, with Sabina going through several medical examinations.

My mother, who was in Pittsburgh to help us during this difficult time, was visiting the United States for the first time in her life. This was also her first trip to any Western country. While she was here, she battled language and culture barriers, both socially and at the hospitals. Her family and in-laws had surrounded her while she delivered her own children. She had taken care of the newborns while household servants cooked food for flocks of friends, relatives and family who would come to see and welcome her newborns with boxes of *mithai* in hands. The maids took care of loads of baby laundry.

My mother found the craziness of our lives in the US overwhelming. I was on my feet, running errands the first day I returned home with Sabina. We were new to Pittsburgh and barely knew anyone apart from a couple of families. I was still in the process of learning to drive, which limited access to the external world and people. Having previously lived in megapolises like Karachi and Chicago, I had never felt the need to drive. Pittsburgh's lack of public transportation made it imperative for me to learn. At the time Ami visited, one of our few entertainments was to hail a cab in the afternoons to visit the nearby Parkway Central Mall in the Greentree neighborhood of Pittsburgh. The mall reflected the despondence and financial blight Pittsburgh was going through at that time, but still provided some respite from the drill of cooking and laundry at home.

In March 2006, Ami had already been diagnosed with an early onset of Parkinson's disease. She needed regular medication and a lot of rest. She had arranged to carry the former with her from Pakistan, but it was not easy to get rest in a two-bedroom apartment with a newborn. I was in post-partum recovery and Sabina's hospitalization right after birth had exhausted me. Bilal did not have time off until two weeks, when Sabina was supposed to be originally born.

During those initial few weeks, my mother, despite her failing health, did what all mothers do and what I was expected to be doing henceforth. She took care of all of us, bringing us home cooked food during the two hospital stays and taking care of Sabina at night so Bilal and I could catch some sleep. We had Sabina's *aqiqah* on the fourteenth day of her birth, when according to the Islamic tradition her head was shaved, and a goat was sacrificed, and meat distributed among the needy to protect the baby from evil eye. The custom dictated that the baby's hair be floated in a nearby river, but we decided against polluting the Monongahela. My mom was disappointed once again and prayed for Sabina's long healthy life despite her parent's superfluity. Later that month we had a small welcome party for Sabina in our Crane Village Apartment. We cooked tons of *Desi* food for a few American friends who were mostly Bilal's colleagues. After spending a month in Pittsburgh, Ami returned to Pakistan, leaving us with a fridge stuffed with kebabs to last us a lifetime. Only, we finished them in two weeks.

Those early days with Sabina were hard. I desperately missed the family support I would have, had I been in Pakistan. "Don't drive, don't climb the stairs, rest enough!" I had heard the preaching many times to new mothers in the family. In my home country, a new mother and her baby were kept in a sanctuary, well-fed and loved for forty days. Sometimes the mother and the baby would even reside at the maternal grandparents' house for the first forty days of childbirth. This was considered essential for the mother-newborn bonding as well as for nurturing the mother in the new role she had to undertake. Special postpartum foods known to expedite the flow of breast milk and provide nutrients for the nursing mother are lovingly prepared by the family and would comprise the new mother's palate in Pakistan.

The reality of my life in Pittsburgh was different. I had to cook, clean and take care of mounds of baby laundry. Sabina was colicky and followed an erratic sleep schedule. I had heard that children brought parents closer, but I started becoming skeptical of this notion during early days of having a child. It felt like Bilal and I were drifting apart, silently battling our personal pressures. It was hard to provide for endless diapers and formula milk on a medical fellowship's stipend, and my husband would sometimes take on extra night shifts to make some money. Sometimes, because of Bilal's busy schedule, I emotionally felt like a single parent. As first-time immigrant parents, we were scared of babysitters, day care or any other person who would expose our child to "external" influences.

I come from a tight-knit culture, where parents have the full responsibility of raising a child. Unlike America, where doctors, schools and social services are all partners in raising a child, Pakistani parents raise a child with full authority, believing that they know the best. My family would often laugh when I told them about the conversations I had with Sabina's pediatrician about her growing palate. Even physicians in my family believed that a child should eat what her parents feed her. "What role does a pediatrician have in it?" My family in Pakistan would question me as I carefully started my daughter on cereal and later Gerber baby food, closely monitoring vegetable and fruit intake.

Sabina was a physically active child and started crawling when she was four months. Our apartment needed "childproofing," another concept that my mother back home could not offer any help with. She had raised her children in an extended family, where there was always someone to keep an eye or hold her children. In Pakistan, childcare was cheap and affordable as well, and all that was expected of the babysitter was to follow the child and keep him or her out of harm's way as the child carried on with excursions. By the time I realized that I needed child locks for my kitchen cabinets, Sabina had already found a favorite hobby in taking out all the pots and pans and playing with them.

Socializing with the limited *Desi* population of Pittsburgh provided some respite. We carved out a place for ourselves among the growing members of "moderate" Muslims, who lay somewhere in between the ultra conservatives and those who had completely assimilated and adapted to the Western culture. Meanwhile, we also knew people on both the extremes. We had acquaintances who arranged their children's marriages at the age of eighteen, before going to college, while many others had children in their thirties still waiting for the spark to happen. As we had our first daughter, all our friends endowed us with their wisdom on raising the perfect Muslim child in America. Many times, the boundaries between religion and culture were blurred and the focus was more on raising a child whose exceptional moral upbringing could be touted in Pakistan.

The story of Sabina's life was written before she was born. In our perfect fantasy world, she was going to speak immaculate Urdu. That was going to be her language of choice. She would never wear short shorts and would love to wear shalwar kameez. She would happily go to an Islamic Sunday School on weekends and have a wide network of *Desi* girlfriends which would naturally eliminate any wrong American influences like making boyfriends. Sleepovers, non-chaperoned trips to the mall or movies were out of the question. Prom was unthinkable. She was going to be a Perfect-Pakistani-Muslimah and at the age of twenty was going to marry a Perfect-Pakistani-Muslim-Man, arranged for her by us, her parents, after an extensive research of her partner-to-be's genealogy. Sabina's life and fate were sealed.

Unbeknownst to us as first-time parents was the fact that as our daughter grows older, she would have a mind and personality of her own. Sabina was rambunctious and full of energy. She showed early signs of being a master of her own universe. She whirled around the house, library, Children's Museum of Pittsburgh, doctor's office or wherever the world would take her. She was curious, smart and quick to grasp the differences between the four walls of her home and the world that existed outside it. She would grow up to ask us: "If Pakistanis always want to meet other Pakistanis and eat Pakistani food, why did they leave Pakistan?" We, her parents, had no answer to that.

Sabina started preschool at the age of two-and-a-half years. It was the first day of *Ramadan* in 2007. From that initial experience of sitting in the waiting area of Sabina's preschool, Mushroom Family Learning Center in Mount Lebanon, until today, school visits have always reminded me of my "otherness." On that first day of Sabina's school, I had to explain to the congenial school staff several times that I could not eat or drink because I was fasting. Over the course of years, I would volunteer at school Field Days while fasting in summer, going without water or food for the day. We even attended a curriculum night held one Eid al-Adha, one of the two biggest Muslim holidays. These instances were a constant reminder that the mention of Muslim holidays on school calendars, was to reflect diversity in the school district but had not led to inclusion.

Just like I had expectations of the American educational system, schools also demanded a lot from me. It was relearning of a different kind in which I was the student and Sabina was my teacher. In the US schools, no one called the principal or teachers Ma'am and Sir, which was how the teachers were addressed at schools in Pakistan. There was no uniform. Both the preschools and public schools in the United States lacked formality that were part of the British inspired educational system in Pakistan. They required parental involvement, parent volunteers in different capacities and had expectations from parents. Here in America, school and family were two important partners in a child's upbringing. I, on the other hand, had grown up in a culture where what happened in school stayed at school and the dichotomy of school and home never crossed boundaries. After all these years, I still remember an instance that defined my future reactions to anything that took place between kids from school, and my own children even outside of school's boundaries.

When Sabina was in second grade, she once had a trivial argument with another girl in her grade who used to ride the same bus as hers. Since the argument was on the bus, it did not occur to me that it needed to be brought up with the girls' class teacher. The next day, I received a call from school, reporting the "incident" to me, along with many accusations made against my daughter. At that time, I found myself at a loss, since I was going through a process of consoling my own child at home, but never thought that I needed to "report" to school whatever happened with her on the bus.

Though Sabina acclimatized to her preschool from day one, my learning curve was steeper. Pittsburgh was snug. Most parents knew each other from their own high schools. At the Valentine's Day and Halloween parties, while volunteer parents talked about common friends and wine nights together, I would mostly resort to looking busy while shuffling through the party supplies of bags of glue and googly eyes. It was also at the school parties that I became familiar with a wide array of American snacks, that I had never considered worth snacking before such as string cheese, pretzels and Chex Mix.

Bilal and I started learning the nuances of the American educational system, the differences between the "good" and "bad" school districts. For many immigrants, education has been their ticket out of their countries. They were able to live and make it in the United States not because of the accident of their birth but by the acquired virtue of education. Academics, as such, are a priority in many first generation immigrant families. For *Desi* immigrants in the generation before mine, education had a single purpose, and that was, to land their child in a medical school. My generation has added a few other "respectable" professions like law and Silicon Valley inspired IT careers to the list. If mothers of Chinese origin in America pride themselves on being tiger moms, *Desi* women are no less than the cheetahs. Many, like myself, had forsaken their own education and aspirations at the altar of supporting husband's careers and raising children. Our competitiveness was reborn through our sons and daughters.

Bilal and I were no different. Alina was born in 2009 and we were parents to two girls. Unlike our first born, Alina was a quiet baby. She allowed me time to recoup from pregnancy and birth, with her conveniently alternating routine of feeding in every three hours and going back to sleep. She was born at another busy time of many new beginnings in our lives of homeownership and extensive paperwork for permanent residency status that leads to the coveted "green card." Bilal also completed his four years long fellowship training the month Alina was born and was offered an attending physician position at UPMC Children's Hospital.

This time around, my mother-in-law, Faizia Sitwat, whom we call Amma, was there to help us run the gamut of chores from the hospital to the house. She also stayed home and took care of Sabina while I was in the hospital to deliver the baby.

Unlike Pakistan, where an entire family can live in one room, here in America, every child craved and needed his/her own space. Long-term guests from Pakistan, who would occupy parts of our house for several days to months, were also the reality of our lives. We purchased a newly built townhome in the prestigious North Allegheny School District where the bar for competition was high given the growing number of Asian and *Desi* students. This suburban community was "safe" and there was none better for our family.

In addition to the school district, there was another big motivator of our move to Wexford in the North Hills of Pittsburgh. The Muslim population was growing in the North of Pittsburgh, and many Muslim families were now choosing to live in the North Hills. Plans for a mosque in the Northern suburbs of Pittsburgh with a Sunday school for kids were underway. There was no doubt in our minds that our kids would attend the weekend Islamic School. In our imagination, we had enrolled them even before they were born.

As immigrants, Bilal and I had no idea as to the reason or purpose of Sunday school. There was no such thing in Pakistan. Islamic Sunday schools were an essentially American institution founded with a purpose to uphold religious and cultural values of the Muslim traditions in America. They were modeled after church schools, filling in gaps in religious instruction that a secular public education system might sometimes create. Islamic Sunday Schools differed from the church weekend schools because they utilized the rigorous model of schooling emphasized in many Muslim countries of South Asia, Middle East and Africa. Like churches and synagogues, they focused on moral and social networking as well as bringing together brothers and sisters in faith from a young age. Though larger mosques across the United States had developed more professional models, Pittsburgh's Islamic Sunday Schools were still hugely volunteer run, with many parents serving in different academic and administrative positions.

At most Islamic Sunday Schools, English was the language of instruction, but Arabic was taught as a language of choice. This never sat well with the *Desi* community and had been responsible for many not-so-congenial situations, especially between Arabic language instructors at the Sunday School and Urdu speaking parents. When a child like mine, who belonged to a South Asian household, brought home Arabic homework, with questions in Arabic that neither she nor I would understand, Google would be our only friend. Some Sunday School administrations in mosques around the United States had opted to teach Urdu, Turkish, or another language of the community's choice in addition to Arabic and mitigate hard feelings. None of the Pittsburgh-area mosques adopted this practice.

By 2014, I had two daughters enrolled in the North Allegheny School District and Muslim Association of Greater Pittsburgh's (MAP) Sunday school in Gibsonia, Pa. Life was crazy. Our two daughters, in elementary school, had busy schedules packed with math enrichment at Kumon, swimming, tennis and tests at Sunday School. During our initial years of parenting, Bilal and I never questioned the *Desi* wisdom. All kids we knew went to Kumon after school. All families went to Sunday School. Sunday school homework and competitions were the topics of conversation at the *Desi* parties. My children started memorizing long chapters of the Quran that I never did growing up in Pakistan. Their rote learning was rewarded at the end of school year graduation with special positions and prizes awarded to those who did well.

North Allegheny School District was an epitome of competitiveness. Many new families, especially those of Asian descent had been making the North Hills of Pittsburgh home, driven by the same qualities that attracted us. We all wanted the best of America at the cheapest cost, and the Northern suburbs of Pittsburgh were still able to provide it unlike urban centers of the region. The school district had a robust Gifted Program in addition to enrichment classes in math and English Language Arts (ELA). Parents strived to get their children into these accelerated programs from the first day at school. I remember a conversation with Sabina's first grade teacher at my first parent-teacher conference, in which she patiently explained to me that though my daughter was smart and might have averaged above 90 percent in each subject, the academic criteria for GOAL testing at North Allegheny School District demanded a 99 percent in each subject. This knocked out my hopes of ever belonging to the elite group of Asian and *Desi* parents at NASD who constantly chatted about their kids GOAL commitments.

My kids had a knack for putting things in perspective for me. With their naïve yet deep comments and questions, they always forced me to ponder over situations from their perspective. As the girls grew older, they started finding conflict in what they saw at home and their time at Sunday school. My 5-year-old Alina refused to cover her head with *hijab* for the Sunday school yearbook because at home, she was encouraged not to be part of something just because others were doing it. A seven- year- old Sabina would wonder how some Muslims ate Big Mac and others didn't. And they both were full of questions about Allah and His powers. If He is all-forgiving why are Muslims so concerned about going to Hell? If we can pray to *Allah* in any language, why must we learn to read the Quran in Arabic?

The highlight of our lives, or perhaps mine, was to visit Pakistan with our children. Both Bilal and I desired the same intimate relationship with grandparents for our children that we had experienced ourselves. We would mostly visit during the winter break, were there when both my brothers got married and aligned our trips with holidays whenever possible. Our trips to Pakistan were great learning experiences, at all ends. Bilal would seldom accompany us and most of the time I would brace the twenty-four-hour journey with the girls on my own. As Ami's Parkinson's progressed, it became almost impossible for her to travel and increased my desire to spend more and more time with her.

The preparations for our trip would start several months before the actual journey, with vaccinations for malaria. Though many Pakistani families were inundated with requests with all kinds of gifts of cosmetics, handbags and shoes from their visiting American families, mine and Bilal's families only coveted large bottles of vitamins and Tylenol in Costco-sized packaging. This, along with cans of formula milk and Pedialyte, invariably made meeting the airline luggage weight requirements an act of juggling.

Nonetheless, every year or so, I would stuff bags with vitamins, over the counter medications and things my American kids would not be able to survive without, such as, Off insect repellent spray, Hydrocortisone and Benadryl, and brave the Pakistan trip.

Once we arrived in Pakistan, our family would be at the airport to welcome us. Sometimes there would be as many as ten people to greet us. They would bring several cars, so it was not a problem to transport our average-sized luggage, that consisted of five to six suitcases. As everyone hugged and greeted, my children would act like zombies, whose brains and eyes had stopped functioning by that time, because of lack of sleep and binge-watching inflight entertainment for the past twenty-four hours.

Our trips usually lasted two to three weeks and from the first day, my kids would fall into a horrible pattern of sleeping the day away and waking up during late hours of the night. This, however, did not bother most of our Pakistani relatives as we are not prone to excessive scheduling. We believe in letting our day and lives flow in the hope that they would eventually find a purpose. Also, not everyone's life would find a purpose, and that would be fine too. Given that philosophy, there is a loosely structured concept of time and spending it "efficiently" in our culture. A good use of time is how you would like to spend it, and if that happens to be sleeping, so be it.

My girls loved their Pakistan trips. They were spoiled to the hilt by their grandparents, aunts and uncles. Over the years of visiting, they developed a taste for spicy cuisine and had snacking favorites like *masala fries* from street vendors. They loved camel and horse rides on the beach and spending time with cousins. They were amused and annoyed at the same time by the traffic patterns devoid of any order or lanes, shared by a variety of vehicles that included cars, rickshaws, motorcycles, trucks, buses, donkey carts and some unnamed hybrid vehicles that were a product of necessity and creativity.

"Real" Pakistanis found my daughters equally amusing, with their lilting Urdu and constant complaints about the hot weather during the winter months in Karachi. My Alina especially would spend most of her time clad in shorts, enclosed in an air-conditioned room, and still complained about the heat. Despite our efforts and generous use of mosquito repellents, the girls would get big red mosquito bite marks on their face and body. Their daily bedtime ritual, that included prayers, had a special request added during our Pakistan trip, that was for *Allah* to save them from "the bites of mosquitoes, bugs and any other things." The irony was that as soon as the girls settled in, it would be time for us to go back home. The home, for all of us including myself, had come to mean the United States of America.

In this way, Islam for my girls became a live religion, and Allah an entity they could look up to with a faith to resolve their little problems. My girls mostly questioned their faith and identity not as a means of getting away from it but as a way of arriving at it with full understanding. Their American schooling had prepared them to be analytical and question what they doubted. Some practices, which were more culturally Muslim than religious, bothered them more. Many of them, like the dress code, had been an important part of my own upbringing in a Muslim country. As my girls waddled on this path of discovery, I tagged along with them. Before I was tasked to raise these American Muslims, my world was safe, my bubble filled with people who looked, talked and dressed like me.

Both my daughters played sports and wanted to wear shorts. My twelve-year-old, at the age when many Muslim girls started considering taking Hijab, declared that she couldn't excel in squash unless she played it in shorts. She was the social butterfly of our house. Everyone at school was her best friend, except for those who were her worst enemies. She was dramatic and temperamental and announced to me one day that she has her dad's permission to choose the boy she would marry. Her weekends started filling up with sleepovers, movie nights and mall trips with friends. She took pride in her squash and relentlessly trained for it with her dad and his friends. She set high goals and standards for herself in everything she did.

I had grown up in a hierarchical culture where parents and adults commanded utmost respect. We never addressed any adults, which included our friends' parents with their first or last names and called them uncle or auntie. I was an auntie to all my desi friends' children. But Sabina's friends called me Mrs. Sitwat. Some would also call me Saima. When her friends were there, we the parents almost functioned in the background, "giving them their space." This was unlike our own youth in Pakistan, where our parents occupied the center stage of the house while we, the children, worked hard to find space in nooks and crannies.

Muslim parents dread the fourth grade in American public schools. It is time for their baby to lose innocence and attend the notorious developmental class that the schools must offer mandatorily as part of the curriculum from fourth grade onwards. Though fourth grade curriculum goes only as far as using deodorant and hitting puberty, for Muslim parents, it's no less than talking about sex. And no good Muslim ever talks about sex. God forbid if such a "movie" was ever shown at our schools in the Muslim world.

As parents have the option to view screening of the video that the kids would be watching, and based on that decide if they felt that their child was ready to face the harsh realities of life or not, I opted to go for the screening that the North Allegheny School offered. I was going with an open mind, that is to watch the film. The decision, like many others in Sabina's life, was already taken when Sabina started kindergarten. It was made in light of the best practices laid down by American Muslim social norms and community preferences.

At the screening, I sat in a room full of like-minded concerned parents. Never before since moving to America had I seen so many people who looked like me in one room. It was a Muslim fest with a few other very concerned parents. Not once did I question my pre decided notions as I watched the hazy video which did a poor job of explaining whatever it was intended to convey. As soon as it ended, school administrators in the room were bombarded with aggressive questions by angry parents, who believed that the school was stealing their children's innocence, at an age when they were far from puberty, which was a personalized fact. The district administrators, who were veterans at this conversation, having held it year after year, were quick to absolve themselves of all responsibility. If they had the option, they would have stayed away from such profanity. But they were mandated by the PA Department of Education to offer developmental classes to their students.

The video was to be shown at the end of a day, the date for which was announced in the beginning of the school year. We had the option of picking up our child earlier that day, if we did not want them to be part of the developmental program. I was one of the proud parents who duly did that and saved my nine-year-old from undue exposure to adult content.

Sabina was surprised that I would be picking her up from school before closing time. I concocted some lame explanation which I could see my child was smart enough to know was untrue, but she happily took her early dismissal from school and did not probe any further. Next day, she informed me that she heard from her friends that she missed an important class at school, which was full of useful information. At that point I told her that I did not want her to be in that class. Sabina's response to this was: "But why, *Amma*? The class was just about sex."

Never again would I go through the trouble of early dismissal and keeping my daughter away from any other developmental classes through grade school.

Sabina was feisty and from her early years looked like a force to reckon with. But it was Alina's "Americanism" which confused as well as fascinated me. Where had this girl come from? From her light skin, to light brown hair and eyes, Alina looked nothing like our South Asian family. She was a perfect product of her country of birth, took pride in wearing red, white and blue every Fourth of July and Veterans Day and swore allegiance to hamburgers and chicken nuggets. Having spent full days at the daycare since she was six-month-old, while I took GRE and then attended graduate school, Alina was at one with the people around her. Even as a baby, she followed schedule to a fault, which was definitely not something that she inherited from her Pakistani genes. Despite her desire to speak Urdu, her train of thought in English was too fast for whatever little patience she had. She barely learned to speak her mother tongue. She found her passion in arts, music and video gaming and her aspirations vacillated between becoming an architect and the President of the United States of America.

Alina was a gifted child. Not only was she formally accepted into the schools' gifted program, every aspect of her life displayed it. At the age of nine, she loved quoting Alexander Hamilton and William Shakespeare. Her love for trivia and magic tricks made her admirable for grown-ups whose company she seemed to enjoy more than her peers. She and her friends would sit down for a board game or cards and play it quietly for hours. Even when left to herself, Alina had the capacity to teleport to the world of books, television and movies, with her favorite Costco chocolate chip mini muffins by her side.

As a mother, I was astonished how two children of the same gender and genetic makeup can be so different from each other. I marveled at the beauty of creation as I saw them growing up, from learning to speak to developing habits, likes and dislikes. Like all parents, I desired that they both reached their full potential in life, doing what they thought was best for them. Despite differences, the girls had things in common. They both loved ice cream and liked squash, sharing a passion for it with their dad. They watched the movie "Boss Baby" gazillions of times and would still not get tired of it. Like all parents of my generation, I had battles to fight over electronics, screen time and social media.

Another thing that both Sabina and Alina had in common was their love for religion in a personal rather than an organized way. I saw it as they prayed every night with a faith in the power of the Almighty. Unlike I expected, they found religion at home, instead of the mosque, through readings of the Quran in English since Arabic memorization did not make sense to them. They found comfort in Islam through curiosity, not resignation, through a kinder, forgiving God. For them, Allah was an entity that would grant their wishes and help them excel in their common pursuits. Both Sabina and Alina had a desire to follow religion through self-discovery, rather than dictated to them from the altar.

I, as a mother, committed myself to guiding my children through their spiritual journey. I started studying Islam in a way that the accident of my birth never required. I had to answer questions that had never occurred to me, growing up in a country where 99 percent of people worshipped my God and followed the same scripture that I did. Now, I had to answer questions such as why didn't Muslims eat pork? "My friend said Jesus is the savior. Is that correct?" "How about Prophet Muhammad?" "Are marshmallows *halal*?" One day, in 2015, my then nine-year-old asked me, "Are Muslims terrorists?"

Motherhood gave me ownership of my religion in a way I never had before. My generation of Muslim parents had the unique challenge of combating *Islamophobia* in schools, in addition to the usual humdrum that all children bring to life. Most immigrant communities to the United States had battled accusations of being "the others" at some point in history, with conspiracy theories abounding their raison d'etre on the American soil. *Islamophobia*, "the fear, hatred of, or prejudice against, Islam or Muslims" was based on the pretext that Muslims are trying to take over America and aim to install *Sharia* Law. The fear had pervaded the American society and the idea that "All Muslims are terrorists" was rampant in my children's America. The idea and imagery were perpetuated by the media and exploited by the politicians.

"Muslim in this country has become a bad word," said Simran Jeet Singh, a senior religion fellow at the Sikh Coalition, while contributing thoughts to a report on "Hate in America," a project of The Center for Public Integrity, published in 2018. Every election cycle since 9/11 has spiked hate crimes against Muslims, with 2016 being the worst in 14 years, during the candidacy of Donald J. Trump. Unfortunately, that was also the first election that my girls were old enough to follow. As the crowds chanted to Trump's calls for the Muslim Ban, my girls like many others tried to make sense of their world and of their country. My ten-year-old Sabina, in fifth grade at that time, had to take ownership in explaining her religion and ethnicity to other kids in class, who thought of all Muslims as ISIS. My daughter had to carry the burden of being a Muslim in this country from a young age, with news of head scarves pulled off from girls and calls of "go back home" traveling across the country. Though I empowered my children with wisdom and knowledge, I feared for them: for a time when they would not have the patience to be polite, when they might lose it or just become tired of giving explanations.

There were incidents at the school and the community that started defining our relationship with both of them, as well as with our own religion. One such story stands vivid among others. In 2018, North Allegheny School District contracted with a local self-proclaimed, self-defense agency, called INPAX, to provide active-shooter training to the faculty, staff and students, across its schools. There was not a thorough vetting process and the district remained silent when questioned about the solicitation of proposal requests.

One of the district parents, Katie Melson Leslie, did some dig and discovered several anti-Muslim, anti-Semitic and xenophobic posts on the owner's personal as well as the business's Facebook page. One of these posts, from the Clarion project, claimed that the American mosques were terrorist camps and identified their locations. A few others poked fun at the LGBTQI community. There were several other posts that not only perpetuated the myth of Muslims as ruthless killers of innocent Americans, but also did much in the way of inciting hatred for other minorities.

In 2018, the North Allegheny School Board consisted of all white members, which was highly unrepresentative of the district's growing diversity. The school board brushed off Katie's efforts to contact and seemed apathetic to her concerns.

Katie did not give up. To say the least, Katie created a movement. She formed a grassroot alliance, which included school district parents, community leaders and partners. She wrote to many of the area mosques, and the one she sent to the Muslim Association of Greater Pittsburgh landed in my inbox. I lobbied not only Muslim friends, but also wrote to the parents of my girls' friends from school.

We all showed up at the school board's working session on April 18, 2018. We had called the media and anyone else who mattered. I had never previously seen so many cars in the administration building's parking lot. The Muslim community of the North Hills of Pittsburgh had shown up to speak and influence the board to revoke its decision. But the real difference was made by our allies. They came from all zip codes of Pittsburgh. They included social justice advocates, lawyers and marketing professionals. For more than two hours, we all worked together and spoke on a stringent schedule of two to five minutes each to convince the board of our point of view. We all invoked the school board members from our personal positions, as mothers, fathers and community advocates. One person simply encouraged the board to do soul-searching and ask their conscience if they were doing the right thing. My then eight-year-old Alina had sent a personally handwritten note to the board about how saddened she was to see people use the word Muslims and terrorists interchangeably, and she hoped that her school would hold a person who does so accountable. "How can we expect children to not say bad things, if adults would do it all the time? Bullying is not funny," Alina wrote.

The owner of INPAX, Sam Rosenberg, was also present in the audience and was one of the last ones to speak. He had previously justified his actions and comments on his posts as depictive of his humor "as a marine." But, that night, Rosenberg was a different person. A handful of people, including one of his employees, had spoken that night on his behalf. But according to Rosenberg, sitting through the speeches and comments made by the speakers, he had a moment of reckoning. He apologized for his actions and offered his availability to meet with the aggrieved parties or anyone concerned.

The day after, North Allegheny School District and INPAX issued a joint statement terminating their contract.

That was a day of celebration for Muslims and their allies not only in the North Allegheny School District but across the Pittsburgh region. The school already upheld its high standards and had just taught several valuable lessons to its students by their decision. You should never bully people. Be careful with social media. When a mistake is made, it has to be rectified. It can't be let go. Students across the district talked about this on their bus rides for days.

Though the INPAX episode brought me a small victory, it also exposed me further to Pittsburgh's deeply set alliances. Some of our friends from school had family members who knew Rosenberg socially. He had provided self-defense training for Girl Scout troops and those groups felt indebted to him. For many others, it became an issue of partisan politics. Rosenberg owned a gun shooting range in McCandless and some folks wanted to wrap the whole thing in the garb of Second Amendment rights. There were also some, I could tell, who thought immigrants like me should quietly live in this country. Were we not happy just to be in America and have the privilege to send our children to good schools? How dare we mess with the policies?

It was for my children that I started reading and writing about Muslims and Islam. It became a formative part of my own life. I had to step outside the bubble of *Desi* parties, where we cried on our problems over a cup of *chai*. Our kids deserved a better world and we needed to have a unified voice to convey our message of peace. The Muslim community existed just as one pillar in the silos of Pittsburgh and needed a unified voice and platform for different communities across Pittsburgh to see and mingle with us. Muslim Association of Greater Pittsburgh (MAP) provided that platform for many others and myself.

. 5 .

MUSLIM MATTERS

"Islam will be what Muslims make of it. And it is the sum total of the interpretation that Muslims give it."

-Maajid Nawaaz, British activist and radio presenter

At the time when my daughters attended Sunday school at MAP, in Gibsonia, Pa., I started volunteering with the school administration as well as the mosque's outreach team. The Arabic word for mosque is *masjid* (plural, masajid). American mosques or masajids, like churches, are mostly community led and driven. The Sunday school required parents to volunteer in multiple capacities, as teachers, lunch helpers, office administration and security personnel.

In keeping with the trend visible across the country as well as in other parts of Pittsburgh, the founding of MAP was to be credited with the growth of the Muslim community in the North Hills of Pittsburgh. Its membership had grown from a handful of founding members in 2011 to over two hundred members in 2018. In addition to these members, there were several hundred non-members who attended the mosque sporadically, on holidays and for Friday prayers.

MAP Sunday School provided a safe space not just for children but also for the adults. It was a Muslim's dream come true. In this microcosm, time spent at the mosque was an outward show of religiosity. It elevated a family's status in the eyes of other community members. Let's say that the amount of time a family spent at the mosque, was considered directly proportional to their proximity to heaven.

The *masjid* was a safe haven where the community could bring the baggage of their external existence as Muslims in America and unload it. It provided a *halal* world for themselves and their children, a place where they could eat everything, *hijab* was the norm and most people were brown. Once the MAP community grew, it would come to be known as a widely South Asian mosque, much to some people's dislike. As the Muslims across the United States struggled for their inclusion in mainstream society, many of our community members found themselves existing on the fringes of their own *masajids* and community organizations, just because of their decision to attend a particular masjid. Mosques across the United States were deemed Arab, Turkish, South Asian and Black, based on the ethnicity of the majority of their congregation members. It was a battlefront, where each Muslim was fighting internal as well as external stigmas associated with being a Muslim in America.

The interfaith and outreach committees had evolved as important components of masjid boards, as the American Muslims worked to shed myths and dispel propaganda. The very tragic attack on the World Trade Center in 2001 had left all American Muslims "presumed guilty", not only to the non-Muslim Americans, but even to themselves to some extent. They realized the harm they had done to their own community, by not developing a collective voice or deeper alliances. A few Muslim organizations that existed before 9/11 had focused on the foundation of mosques and resolving their internal disputes rather than advocacy and building community partnerships with people of other faiths.

For Muslims in the United States, "It was the best of times, it was the worst of times." Outwardly, the odds seemed against us, but many people across America had heard the words "Muslim" and "Islam" for the first time. It might not be for the reasons we would be proud of but still during this time, Islam and its followers were at the forefront of American living rooms and dining tables. Muslims, a people who had existed in American neighborhoods for hundreds of years, were overnight turned into exotica. All of a sudden, these Muslims came to be recognized as different, people who needed to be studied and understood and not just hung around with. America needed Muslims to explain themselves. Nowhere in history this need had been more apparent than during the years leading up to the presidential election of 2016.

The American mosques braced to fulfill this gap to the optimal. In an effort to rebrand, mosques across America opened their doors to people of all faiths and concentrated their efforts on building bridges and interfaith relations. This rebranding, however, was a double-edged sword. It opened mosques to new vulnerabilities and challenges at a time when people doubted good intentions. It exposed these previously isolated spaces, not only to unfriendly visitors but also FBI sting operations. It created internal rifts within the Muslim community, where mosque administrations and outreach committees were often criticized for recruiting a certain "brand" of Muslims to do their work. At MAP, in 2015, the outreach and social services team consisted mostly of women.

Though the interfaith and social services inspired me, administration became my forte at MAP. My academic background in strategic planning and public policy along with Barb's mentorship had provided me a vision of running public and nonprofit enterprises. In 2015, the year Trump and Hillary Clinton declared their respective candidacies, I was elected to serve as MAP's Executive Secretary.

American mosques are an American product, vividly distinct from mosques in the Muslim countries. In my native country Pakistan, mosques, excluding a few large ones, were places for men to pray. They did not serve any other purpose beyond that. But, in the United States, far from the ritualistic practices of Muslim homelands, the institution of mosque had evolved in the same tradition as the original concept, developed and perfected by the Prophet Muhammad (peace be upon him) during the earlier days of Islam. The creation of the American mosque was also inspired by the model of churches and synagogues, to serve as places of communal gatherings. Most places of worship in America shared characteristics and were almost identical apart from the faiths they represented. They all served congregants, with a growing number of them questioning the value of faith and God in their lives. They were also all rife with internal groupings and social politics, as I had already heard from my veteran counterparts. MAP, as I would come to realize, was not excluded from this flaw. Before I knew it, I was entangled in the labyrinth of social hierarchy that determined our roles on MAP's Executive Council (EC).

From the onset, I was an outsider in this world of organized religion. My husband and I had grown up in households that consisted of educators, doctors and engineers. Our families had practiced a mild version of *Sunni* Islam for generations, where we were taught to observe the basic tenets of our religion, but disregard rituals. Much like the educated elite of any religion, we were taught to stay away from religious discourse and any institution that would lead us into such dangerous territories. My parents' religiosity had never ventured beyond personal into the public realm. Our religious life mostly ended with fasting, praying and charity, never branching into congregating or proselytizing. My two brothers and I were expected and taught to observe religion at our own discretion. In fact, during my days of growing up in Pakistan in the 1980s, my parents took great care that their children did not become "Islamized."

I seldom realized this during my days of youth that my family followed a humanistic, spiritual Islam, which placed importance on expansion of mind and valued deeds rather than rituals. We were raised to be volunteers and contribute to the larger society in whatever meaningful way we could. We were taught and encouraged to use our talents in whatever significant ways we could, not shying away from the challenge at hands. It was with this spirit of service that I signed up to be a part of the leadership team at MAP. Honesty of intention for one's deeds and actions is a cornerstone of Islamic practice. "Verily, all actions are but driven by intention and for everyone is what he intended," narrated a famous *hadith*.

However, as soon as I started my term at MAP, I realized that though the sentiment of service was uniform across the board for all those who committed themselves to MAP, motives to serve were different. Different people had their foot in MAP's door for a multitude of reasons. For some it was a platform to gain social status, worldly and wordy leadership titles, like president, president-elect, treasurer etc. and they reveled in this opportunity. For some others, the mosque was the house of Allah and there was no cause worth serving for or to die for than the cause of Allah. Driven by their religious zeal, they used their influence to socially and politically martyr anyone who disagreed with their idea or brand of Islam. My own time to be counted among such martyrs was not too far. Years later, when a community patriarch pointed out my inability to navigate social politics, I would admit my naivete in signing up to be part of the mosque administration driven by purely altruistic motives.

My first official gig at MAP was to serve in the previously vacant position of executive secretary on MAP's Executive Council. It was the fourth year of our young mosque's creation. Many people, including my husband, warned me of the dangers of stepping into such territories. The outgoing EC members had done a phenomenal job of taking care of the responsibilities of the executive secretary's position, by dividing it among different people. I was quickly filled in and began my work fast.

The governance structure of MAP was laid out with a permanent governing board and an elected Executive Council. In keeping with the Muslim tradition and needs of the time, women were well represented on both these parallel groups. The governing board members served as trustees while the elected council members were to run day-to-day operations of the community center with minimal interference from the trustees. This was what was decided on paper. The reality of who managed what was far from it.

In 2015, all of us were volunteers. The only paid employee our growing organization could hire at that time was a cleaning lady who cleaned twice a week at a discounted rate. EC members took turns to serve as *imam*, office manager and the cleaning crew. During this year, I often thought of what one past President of another mosque, the Muslim Community Center of Greater Pittsburgh (MCCGP) in Monroeville, Pa., had once said to me. "If you want to know where garbage cans are placed in this mosque, all you have to do is to once serve as the president of this place. You would always know where garbage bins are located!"

Though made in a jest, this comment deeply reflected expectations of our community from its elected officials. At our mosque hardly a decision could be made without blessings from the committee of elders in the governing board. The Executive Council members were often tasked with running event logistics, cleaning up after the event, doing inventory of paper products and opening and closing the doors. Overwhelmed by the mundane tasks, at times the EC became an isolated group of individuals who were so engrossed in performing their chores that they lost connection with the greater community. As people came and left for Friday prayers, family nights and Sunday school, the EC members would be busy setting up food, making announcements and acting hosts. When everyone left, we would make sure before leaving that all lights and doors were closed.

However, the year 2015 was a little different. Not many EC members had to worry about the logistics. The President at that time, whom the community affectionately called Ishfaq *bhai*, was usually master of the ceremonies from opening the doors to closing the lights. Between making arrangements, he would sometimes serve as an emcee for the events, on others as the imam leading prayers and on certain occasions as both.

Ishfaq *bhai*'s selfless devotion to MAP was remarkable. His enthusiasm was contagious and inspired all those who worked with him to do their best. The EC members met once a month and continued our work beyond it. Despite his professional and family responsibilities, Ishfaq *bhai* found time to mentor all who sought his help. I became one such mentee.

I was not required to do much during the EC meetings. My role as the executive secretary tied me to taking meeting notes that I quietly did, sitting in a corner. I seldom spoke or was asked to contribute. I was also the youngest member of the EC and it did not look like that my two cents were ever solicited. Most of my work took place before and after the meeting, in sorting MAP's membership database, organizing paperwork and coordinating events.

2015 was an exciting year for the American politics. The Presidential candidates from two dominating parties, Hillary Clinton and Donald Trump, were both unconventional candidates. They turned the political stage into a reality TV show. America became a playground for political pundits around the world. But, as the campaign rhetoric picked up, America started falling apart socially, racially and culturally. Donald Trump put the "Muslim Ban" and "Border Wall" at the center of his "Make America Great Again" slogan. The Republican candidate legitimized hate-speech and bigotry. Xenophobia took off and pervaded the American society with Muslims and immigrants, along with many others caught in the nationalist zest.

As part of my desire to provide more visibility for the Muslim presence in Western Pennsylvania, I had started MAP's first social media page with great enthusiasm. As the election year drew closer, I had to constantly monitor that page for vilifying comments. The comments that would be left on the page ranged from ignorant to purely malicious, sometimes verging on threats to life and property. They called Muslims "unwanted" in the area and left profanc and vulgar remarks on our posts. In response to a picture from a gun control rally that some women from MAP, including myself had attended, comments were left that misquoted Quran by taking Quranic verses completely out of the context. The purpose of these comments was to accuse us, Muslims, of hypocrisy since we were obviously the violent ones. The comments looked completely inappropriate given a photo which depicted five totally non-combative looking women, dressed in western clothes. We could have been any women on the street, if it was not for our facial features or religion. Though I had read and heard about it, I was shocked to personally see this side of America. These people who were now butchering mine and my community's character were until now, my neighbors, friends and colleagues. But the political scenario in 2015 was such that the Republicans, Democrats and everyone in between fell apart on social media. In fact, social media gave everyone a platform where anyone could say the ugliest of things without revealing their identity. In the later years, the divisive role that the social media played during the elections of 2016 would become apparent.

During these troubled years for the American Muslim community, Ishfaq *bhai*, through his example, taught me the role of leadership during tumultuous times. He exercised an almost prophetic calm and kept those on the EC who did not identify with his vision under the radar, with a unique combination of authority and humility. His eyes were always on the big picture of community building, in which daily skirmishes did not matter. Together we worked on simplifying many procedures at MAP. It was Ishfaq *bhai's* vision that later led to electronic management of MAP's treasury, fundraising and membership processes.

Though conservative leaning himself, Ishfaq *bhai* was always open to new ideas, especially when it involved aligning *masajids* and Islamic organizations with other places of worship and nonprofits. It was with this spirit that we hosted MAP's first Volunteer Recognition Event. Each event that I organized helped me learn a thing or two about myself. On a positive note, volunteer recognition taught me the importance of boosting the community's morale. On the other hand, I also realized how little I knew the community I was serving. At a small *masjid* like MAP, everyone was a volunteer. With only one or two employees, the sheer existence of this place was a testament to the exceptional volunteerism of this community. As we recognized and handed out certificates to over seventy volunteers, we certainly disappointed some who were inadvertently left out. The point of contention were a few kids, who had been present at *masjid* while their parents volunteered and had lent a helping hand to their parents. The parents thought that their children should have been recognized as well.

The names of volunteers were submitted by the chairs of our various committees at MAP. But as the emcee of the event, and person on the mic, I looked like the main culprit who had left people out at my sweet discretion. Lessons were learned quickly. As any nonprofit, we could not upset our constituency, especially a few days before the fundraiser. We acknowledged our young volunteers and some other heart-broken souls at a later event. For the next volunteer appreciation dinner, two years later in 2018, I would get several extra certificates printed without any names on them. There were still people who were left out, but this time, we could include them in the ceremony right away. To my delight, the FedEx guy who printed the certificates informed me that he could totally envision a similar episode at his church. He noted the lack of names on a few certificates before he printed them. When I shared the reason with him, he could not stop laughing. "Man! That could totally be at my church. You should write this in a book. We are all so alike!" To hear this in 2018, from a white blue-collar worker, in Trump's America, was music to my ears.

As Ishfaq *bhai's* term drew to a close, it looked almost an impossible task to fill his shoes. The President-Elect at the time, who was to replace Ishfaq *bhai* as the President, was a product of compromise between different community factions. Not only did he not have the sincerity, expertise or temperament to be a community leader, there were also concerns as to the amount of time he could devote to nurturing the community spirit while dealing with external pressures.

The MAP community came together during the Annual General Body Meeting to elect its representatives. Though an official nomination and election system was in place, the "kingmakers", a group that mostly consisted of the big donors and community patriarchs, always had recommendations for some priority candidates to fill leadership roles. In 2016, as the United States of America prepared to elect its first female President, MAP kingmakers successfully convinced their community to elect not only the first female President for their organization, but for any Pittsburgh-area mosque.

It was decided that a woman like me was just what MAP needed at that time. I was an immigrant like the majority of my congregation but had ties across the Pittsburgh region. I had been a fierce advocate for the place of immigrants and Muslims in the American society. Liberal to the core, yet at one with my religion, history and the South Asian culture, I satiated the Muslim community's desire at that time to look pragmatic and make a statement to the rest of the United States that they had elected a female President before anyone else could.

My top leadership role at MAP started a new and different chapter of my life. I had never set foot in a mosque when I landed in Chicago 13 years ago. Who could have thought that one day, the most vivid chapter of my American story would be about a mosque's leadership? As luck would have it, in 2016, I was elected as the President-Elect or Vice President, a role that was to transfer into serving as the President of the Muslim Association of Greater Pittsburgh, in 2017.

. 6 .

IN THE NAME OF ALLAH

"In the end we will not remember the words of our enemies but the silence of our friends."

-Martin Luther King Jr., American minister, civil rights
advocate, Nobel laureate

April 22, 2016, was a happy day. I was elected to be the President of MAP and was to serve a year as the president-elect during 2016-17, mostly shouldering responsibilities as a Vice President that year. There were no counter claims to my nomination. The pride of this accomplishment extended beyond my family and friends. My election did not only make the Muslim women feel empowered, it also pleased community stakeholders, who were mostly men. The collective feeling was one of joyous speculation at the prospect of a female president and what she could do for the image of the Muslim community in Pittsburgh. Some others, as I would later realize, saw a female president as an opportunity to manipulate, dictate and get a free hand at an organization that had thrived on male bonding until then.

My two years, first as the president-elect and then as the president of MAP were a roller coaster ride. I passed through an upheaval of emotions, ranging from paranoia and excitement to deceit and intrigue. Despite the negativity of emotions and actions that would surround us, we continued to be brothers and sisters in faith and called each other so. We never forgot to bestow Allah's blessings on each other, always ending our fury-filled emails and meetings with *Jazak Allah Khair*. In the end we all came out even, together as a community, just as we started out on that April 22.

As Donald Trump and Hillary Clinton took to the national stage, partisan politics became identity politics and gender became our most important identity. The air of the election year made women ambitious and men, carnal. We all aspired to our highest ambition that often reduced us to the lowest level of humanity. The new President of our mosque, and my superior at that time, Zeeshan Ahmed, seemed greatly inspired by Trump and his politics. Candidate Trump had not left any doubts as to his opinion of Muslims as well as his administration's oppressive policies towards us if he got elected. Our mosque's President, however, thought of Trump as a genius who had found ways to play with people's minds and hearts. His inspiration was evident in his impulsive personality and thoughtless decision-making process. Later in the year, we would have several "emailgates" of our own, with the final one targeted at me.

MAP's Executive Council in 2016 was the sixth one for the organization and a first without the presence of a community veteran. For some members, including Zeeshan himself, it was the first time to serve on a nonprofit board. We started without any formal training or introduction to procedural documents and bylaws that could have defined a smooth way forward. It was both liberating and frightening, to be able to, what we thought at that time, make our own decisions without the authoritative resolve of community elders. I would later realize that what had looked like interference at times, was actually diplomatic mediation that kept many tribulations at bay. In the absence of these community veterans, there was no one to ebb the tide and make sanity prevail when the going got tough.

Our chief was a man of whims. He thought of his actions as beyond explanation, especially to women. His spontaneity would have been an asset, if it was exercised with some caution and not according to his personal likes or dislikes. He was a poster child of male patriarchal culture in our mosques, that many women like me were trying to change. He was used to bullying his way around and would not hesitate to tarnish the reputation of those he did not find agreeable, through lies and deceit.

Our EC had a rocky start as Ishfaq *bhai* moved on and the new President took charge. Zeeshan Ahmed thrived on male patriarchy and brotherhood. He was not against women. He was just oblivious to their existence. On one occasion, when I called out on him for leaving me, his next-in-line, out of an important event's planning at the mosque that eventually went awry, he admitted that the thought of including women in making decisions never occurred to him.

We had failed to fill my old position of Executive Secretary during the elections. MAP bylaws provided that if a position is left unfulfilled during election, the EC could nominate a person of their choice to that post, after an internal voting between the EC members. It was therefore up to the new EC to appoint someone as the Executive Secretary.

By the time our EC was getting ready to appoint an Executive

Secretary, I had already realized the importance of having a senior community member at our table, to keep us guided and focused on the service mission of MAP. An esteemed community member, known for his integrity and high regard in the Muslim community of Pittsburgh and among various area mosques, agreed to serve in that position. Zeeshan, however, saw such a person as a threat to his own powers and jurisdiction.

The EC members at that time were open to an internal election, which as the votes looked, would have resulted in the senior member of our community being elected to the EC position. However, what those of us who had joined in the spirit of social good were dismissing was the fact that each of us also comprised one vote on the EC. The only person who could not look past this was our president. He directed all his efforts in creating a voting block which included filling the leftover position with a person whose only qualification was to be the president's best friend.

I, like others on the EC, suggested an election between the two candidates. However, since the President's nominee did not have a good chance of standing up to the other candidate, our chief of staff resorted to horse trading. He first tried to pull that it was predecided by the previous president, Ishfaq *bhai*, as to who would be the next Secretary. When no one bought that argument, he called me personally. When that didn't work, I got a phone call from the community patriarch, Mr. Masood Haq, who had played an important role in my nomination and getting elected.

Haq held several positions at our small organization. In 2016, he was the chair of the governing board, had served multiple roles on the Executive Council until then, chaired the imam oversight committee and several other committees and groups that remiss me at this point. He had situated himself such that not an email could go through MAP's various departments and committees without passing by his eyes. His experience in "managing people" was only matched by his territorial instincts. He had successfully driven all his opponents away from MAP, so all who remained were either his friends, or people of my generation, who were more like wards.

Since the inception of MAP, Mr. Haq had to use only one weapon to always turn the tide in his favor, or as he claimed, in the mosque's favor. This was the threat of "the other mosque." That was all he had to say to me as well, when I received that phone call.

The "other mosque" argument always worked for anyone who had MAP's interest at heart. A few years prior to MAP's creation, some of the mosque's founding members defected from a larger group of Muslim community members, over financial and administrative matters. The original group went on with the construction of the Islamic Center of Northern Pittsburgh which was later renamed the Islamic Center of Western Pennsylvania (ICWP). In 2016, ICWP, continued to actively fundraise to build and open their own mosque, less than five miles from where MAP was situated.

But what's in a name! To most of us who were not part of the original fall out, it was just the "other mosque," a literal white elephant with its white building which had so far engulfed millions of dollars of the Muslim community of Pittsburgh over more than ten years, and still not showed signs of opening its doors, in 2016. Yet, its strategic location and easy access as compared to MAP's, gave many devout a reason to pray for its speedy opening, so they could perform five daily prayers at that premises. The fear of "the other mosque" loomed large over our heads especially at the time of fundraisers and no one exploited it more to his advantage, than Haq, who had an axe to grind with the board president of the "other mosque."

Masood Haq was given many names by the lesser mortals at MAP. Some called him the "Mayor," while others referred to him as the "Godfather." Some just out rightly called him "The Don." His personal grudge with the Board President of the "other mosque", went several years back to incidents at yet another mosque in Monroeville, Pa. Though Haq was not part of the initial defected group, he was not to stay away from the gains of this social experiment and quickly assumed the leadership of MAP and consolidated power in his person as well as the governing board. We all respected him for reasons of traditional male patriarchy, and he used this to his full advantage.

It was Masood Haq who called me one day, advised me to back off, forget about "what's fair" and let the President "have his way!" Though I could see writing on the wall with all of the President's men filling up MAP's EC seats, I had no option but to give in to the hierarchical decision-making. "This is Zeeshan's time, as yours would be next year," Masood Haq told me dismissively. "If you two fight, the community would be divided, and the other mosque's group would get a chance to penetrate." At this decree, I was forced to let slide the candidacy of the senior community member, who was also spoken to separately and made to give up his right to contest. Zeeshan, our president, nominated and got his candidate elected, who in some circles came to be known as his henchman.

And that was just the beginning. It set the tone for the year to come, with men versus women, authority above deliberation and politics and bickering over service. Masood Haq became Zeeshan's anchor and confidante. This made him privy to conversations, which should have been confidential to the EC. And it gave him an opportunity to play the oldest arrow in the sling, that was, the gender card.

I started finding myself always on the losing side, full of doubt, often working like a secretary than a president-elect. Zeeshan Ahmed claimed that he had no time or patience to read "long" emails. I would read all community emails, summarize them for him and rally the summaries to him. I would remind him to write and respond to people's emails and advice with no hopes of ever being listened to. I also had to be an advocate for his leadership, just so that the community does not perceive a dysfunctional EC, a situation that "the other mosque" could always take advantage of. We all trudged along. We were somehow sustaining the internal pressures, but eventually the external events led us all to an emotional breakdown.

In November 2016, the worst nightmare of the Muslim community in the United States of America came true. Donald Trump ascended to the highest office in the country. Mr. Trump wanted to "Make America Great Again." He sought to fulfill this grand idea by attempting to whitewash the country. His hateful ideology and campaign rhetoric had gained him popularity among fascists, Nazis and other extremist factions of the American society. As Trump was elected the president, there were 900 hate crimes against minorities in America within the first ten days, with the highest percentage of them against immigrants, according to The Southern Poverty Law Center. The presidential election came as a major blow to the Muslim community, which felt deceived in its American ideal of "liberty and equality for all." More than anything, was the feeling of being cheated by our neighbors and friends who had sacrificed us as they bought into the narrative of this presumed greatness and prosperity for the country.

It would be an understatement to say that the Muslim community in America belched at the thought of what they saw coming in the era of Trump. We were devastated. Mosque leaders across the United States consulted and organized to protect their communities, who feared whitelash from the extremist factions. Following the election, Muslim leaders with national influence were advising women to disguise their Islamic identity by considering alternative ways of covering head, and not to take *hijab*. It was a time of great despair and also one that required cautious and mindful leadership.

Zeeshan , however, had an unusual calm about security and emotional concerns of the community. Some of us had previously attended an online training conducted by the FBI to ensure security of places of worship. The FBI had advised mosque administrations to build close relationships with their local law enforcement and stay in touch with them. Many of us wanted to send a cautionary word to our local police department at that time, but Zeeshan's suggestion was to pick up arms himself. We disagreed again. The morning after the election, I requested him to send an email to the MAP community to reassure everyone and remind them of the democratic principles America was built and thrived on. Though he initially resisted the idea and deemed it unnecessary, eventually he sent out a message of resilience, which resonated well with most people.

One person on our Executive Council did not agree with this verbiage of "all will be well." This was Yumna, our outreach and social services coordinator for MAP, in 2016. Yumna was born and raised in America unlike most other MAP congregants, and was a perfect picture of an American Muslim woman down to her *hijab*, vernacular and that particular assertiveness that comes only as part of being a "true" American. Civically engaged and politically motivated, Yumna was later criticized for the very attributes which had led to her appointment as the outreach coordinator in the first place.

Yumna had replaced the mighty Masood Haq in this role. Though Mr. Haq moved on from MAP's Executive Council, he refused to transfer the necessary documents and contacts to his successor, so she could take the work forward. As Yumna struggled to find her place within this chauvinist structure dually manipulated by Zeeshan and Masood Haq, she was also thrown back by the election of Donald Trump, like no other person I knew. She had devoted a huge amount of time to campaigning, speaking and advocating on behalf of both the Muslims and the Democratic Party and found it hard to reconcile that her efforts had been in vain. She unraveled, and in the way of her anger ruffled many feathers.

Yumna and Zeeshan Ahmed came from two different worlds. One was a hardcore feminist while another was committed to maintaining the male status quo at the mosque. From the very beginning, they had found it hard to work together as a team, but as grievances accumulated, minor skirmishes culminated in a final blow. Zeeshan's cavalier attitude did not sit well with Yumna. She wanted MAP to send out a firm message, warning the community of impending danger that they were facing now that Donald Trump was elected. She also wanted to hold preemptive training on *Islamophobia*. To all this, Zeeshan said "No."

Then there was the collision. Over a minor and very impersonal decision, Zeeshan and Yumna came head-to-head with each other. They accused and trashed one another on an email thread with eight other people on it. Some of us tried to bring sanity to that conversation, but Zeeshan, encouraged by Masood Haq went too far, accusing Yumna of racism and snobbery, which held no grounds in reality. Yumna resigned. To those who tried to convince her to take her resignation back, she declared that she wanted to focus her energies on fighting the President of the United States of America and not the President of MAP. All was considered "amicably" resolved, at a conflict resolution meeting in a Panera meeting room under the thoughtful mediation provided by Mr. Haq.

That year at MAP was the first time I had personally seen male privilege in action. I was raised in a household where my voice mattered as much as my brothers and male members of the family. My husband and his family were no different. We had our share of differences in life, which had always led us to explore options without one imposing his or her whims on another. During the course of life, I had known men as fellow students and colleagues and always had healthy discourse and conversations with them. But my male colleagues at MAP were different. Not only had I witnessed Yumna and her pride sacrificed at the altar of male ego, I was soon to become a victim of it myself.

The beginning of 2017 was probably one of the darkest times at MAP. President Trump had left no doubts as to his enforcement of the Muslim Ban as one of the first tasks he would complete after assuming office. Our own President Zeeshan Ahmed had joined hands with his cronies, including the governing board chair and other men on the EC to exploit and disregard female voices. Our office manager would not be paid for weeks. She had to remind the treasurer over and again to issue paychecks for herself as well as the cleaning service. She was always disappointed and rebuked by the treasurer who would ask her not to bug him as he had many other "important responsibilities in life." We sat through long, inconclusive meetings, divulged in social politics, sulked often and resolved nothing. Gossip started spreading and the faith of the believers in their elected officials was shaken.

Part of my responsibilities as the president-elect of MAP was to chair the Renovation Committee. Our primary project during my tenure consisted of finishing the building's basement and its conversion into a social hall. It was the first time a woman at MAP had found herself in that role. It was also the first time that Masood Haq was not included on a construction project at MAP, for obvious reasons. He decided to join hands with Zeeshan Ahmed and the rest to make things difficult.

On March 17, 2017, things came to a standstill on various grounds. I resigned from the position of the president-elect for MAP. The bone of contention was the treasurer, who was often out-of-town and failed to fulfill his responsibilities, which among others, included making timely payments to our staff and vendors. When tasked, he would threaten to resign and Zeeshan would talk him back in.

It was decided at an earlier conflict resolution meeting, that the treasurer should leave a few checks, from the restricted use renovation account with me. I oversaw the renovation committee and was also the EC member with most availability at that time. Initially, the treasurer refused to do so, despite his own failure to address accounts in time. Once he was pressed, he left me with unsigned checks. I only realized that those checks lacked the treasurer's signatures that were necessary for acceptance and processing, at the moment I planned to use them, while sealing the deal with the contractor we had selected to work on the construction project. Out of necessity, I gave a signed check from MAP's operations account, instead of the renovation account. This was not a unique situation and many times in the past our treasurers had borrowed and transferred money from one account to another. However, the treasurer endlessly criticized me for my actions verbally as well as through emails. He accused me both publicly and privately. Zeeshan Ahmed played his cards well, or so he thought, by concocting lies at all fronts.

I felt used and exploited. My days were spent on the phone, talking to the community elders, each of whom advised me from their own perspective. I was unable to concentrate on my work or family. I had accepted the position to serve the house of Allah and be an advocate of my faith, but all it had brought to my life was dirty politics. During this time, I won some great friends, avid supporters and worst enemies. I still mourn the loss of some friends who let the lies cloud their judgment. I felt vulnerable and unsure of myself. Inspired by the *Holy Quran*, my own life and upbringing, I often spoke at interfaith events about the elevated status of Muslim women and Islam's emphasis on equality of men and women. However, what I saw in action, at this mosque in Gibsonia, was different. The same people who had earned the title of the most progressive *masjid* in the Pittsburgh area by electing me, would trust a man's words against my own. What did it matter if I was right? I was advised to compromise and stay quiet. It was going to be the men's show and I, the youngest woman at the table, better stay out of the performance. I was heartbroken and dejected. My family felt impacted by my mental fatigue and both Bilal and I thought that I should pull myself out of the craziness around me.

I sent in my resignation to all of MAP's stakeholders, which included the board, EC and Sunday School administration. I also filed grievances in writing, with MAP's grievance committee against the treasurer and his supporters on the EC. My husband, who was also represented on the grievance committee, excused himself from the process.

It brought the community to action. The treasurer also resigned. This time, his resignation was accepted. Many deemed Zeeshan Ahmed's leadership a failure. My well-wishers, which included Ishfaq bhai, Sunday School principal Azra, my dear friend and board member Sabeen and a few others encouraged me to take my resignation back as they tried to "control" the situation. It was already the month of March by then, which meant that there were only three more months left for pulling it through, until the next election. People including the President, Zeeshan Ahmed, himself pleaded and requested me to take my resignation back. After an overwhelming reassurance from all the stakeholders who promised "to make things better," both for myself and MAP, I sent in a note revoking my resignation and continued to serve. I would not have done so had I known that in Zeeshan Ahmed's mind this was a war of egos which he must win.

Despite grievances, the social hall renovation project started. We had raised funds over more than one year and in my opinion our community and especially children deserved a safe space without open wiring and exposed pipes and furnaces. As it would turn out, there was mold found in the basement ceiling, which, as it was discovered in later years, was spread all over the facility. MAP's Annual General Body Meeting and Elections approached amidst low morale with no one ready to join the ranks of what looked like warring factions.

Zeeshan felt coerced into decision-making and took the negotiations as his loss. His masochism felt defeated and, in turn, he would not let me rest. He and his cronies on the Executive Committee started a defamation campaign against me. It was way too easy to see parallels and inspiration from Trump's attacks against Hillary and Zeeshan's against Saima. He tried to kill my "likeability" by projecting me as a strong-willed, ambitious woman, all of which, according to Pew Research, are assets for a man but considered negatives for female leaders. I was projected as careless and callous with the community money. Everything I said was negated and outright ignored. I was dumped with extra responsibilities and then tasked for not executing them well.

I am reminded of one particular incident from those days. There was not much activity at the mosque during weekdays. There were days when there was absolutely no one there. I used to frequent the mosque during daytime, to oversee the social hall construction. During one of these visits, I found a car I had never seen before, parked outside the mosque. It did not belong to any of our construction crew, who were the only people supposed to be there.

Several incidents of vandalism of mosques, including bombings, had taken place in the United States during the years following 9/11 and had especially escalated during the past few months of the election cycle. We had been advised by the US Department of Homeland Security to keep our guards high and not ignore any suspicious activity in or around the mosque. An abandoned car at a time like this looked nothing less than a bomb threat.

My immediate reaction to this was to alert the EC so we could take action right away. Our president first ignored the matter then criticized me for overreacting. However, the women on our EC who mostly chose to remain quiet, sprung to action this time and coerced the President into taking action. Grudgingly, he sent out a community email to verify if the car belonged to one of our congregants. When no one responded to that, the rest was left for me to resolve.

I sought the advice of Kazim *bhai*, probably the eldest member of MAP who was also part of our renovation team. We contacted police, who came and inspected the car and though it was found to be harmless, it could not be verified. The police declared it abandoned and we had it towed away. No one claimed it. It was eventually sent to a dumpster.

As Kazim *bhai* and I saw this car through removal, Zeeshan only watched from the sidelines, expected reporting and always found things to criticize. As his own and his two friends on the EC's terms drew to a close, they all unified under one objective that was to tarnish my reputation with concocted lies. During those days, the community members, sometimes including my friends, often questioned me about things they had "heard." It reminded me of a couplet by a famous Pakistani poetess, Parveen Shakir:

"My honest explanations will lose/ His smart lies will win hearts."

In addition to me, three other women served on the EC. Most were easily won over by Zeeshan's tales, in which he was a helpless man and I, a domineering woman who would not listen to him. He was the community's servant, while I only cared about myself and wasted money. Though it seemed otherwise at that time, as I look back, I can see that most of my female colleagues might not have believed in Zeeshan's earnestness but tagged along so that we could maintain a semblance of functionality. This was how we, the South Asian Muslim women were bred. We never got in the way of a man and his territory, doubly so if that man is angry. Zeeshan's tantrums were working to his advantage.

Amidst this chaos, we approached the day of the general body meeting and elections on April 9, 2017. We were lucky to fill in all the positions with some surprisingly capable community members, who were thorough professionals. Many other MAP members, which included past presidents of the organization, offered help. One offered to assist with the fundraising committee while another chaired the *Eid* Committee, that organized our two big holiday festivals. It was an accomplishment in itself to fill all positions on such a rocky bed.

MAP Executive Council's term runs from July 1 to June 30 each year. The tradition of elections in April provides a transitional time especially of the responsibilities from the president to the president-elect. But, during his last two months in the office, Zeeshan acted as if his term had just started. Instead of transitioning, he concentrated efforts on regrouping. I was not even introduced as the incoming president at the GB meeting. My role and work until then were minimized during the meeting while others including the past treasurer were glorified. During the meeting, I fulfilled the role of executive secretary and checked people in along with the election committee, while the actual executive secretary sat in the front row.

However, this was just a preview of the battle of wills that was to ensue. A significant characteristic of the *Desi* culture and mindset is to sweep things under the rug, without fully addressing or even consciously acknowledging them. The semblance is always of a clean room, since we have a tendency to hide all our garbage.

Most of the MAP community were silent spectators to my plight and blatant disregard. They, however, held no one accountable. It was almost a silent commitment never to socially discuss the ongoing trauma at any *Desi* parties, where I continued to laugh and chat every weekend. Everyone knew what was going on but no one knew how to respond. No one wanted to take sides. The bickering and the bantering were restricted to never-ending email threads and text messaging.

Encouraged by the community's inaction, Zeeshan's malice blossomed. I was deliberately removed from all *Ramadan* arrangements that year and then criticized for staying away. The last attempt by Zeeshan, a few days before his term came to an end, was to have my presentation removed from the program on MAP's Annual Day of Giving. He threatened to boycott the program if this demand was not accepted. Some community stakeholders would convince Zeeshan to attend, but still did not give in to this childlike desire.

This was probably the first time in months when I regained my confidence, stood the ground and refused to attend the fundraiser myself, if I was not to be given a chance to deliver specifics of the basement renovation project personally. Our fundraising chair supported me and agreed. Together, along with our phenomenal keynote speaker Haroon Moghul, for the first time in the history of MAP and many other Pittsburgh-area mosques, we raised more than our fundraising goal of $100,000 in one night. From then onwards, raising more than the annual targeted amount, would go on to become one of the great traditions of MAP. That same night, Zeeshan and his cronies were acknowledged and rewarded with gift cards for their "valuable" contributions and service to MAP. They later made fun of the gifts. What was done in the hope of remedying relations and keeping the community intact backfired and divided us further.

On June 27, 2017, three days before his term was about to end, Zeeshan instituted an ad hoc committee using his "jurisdiction as the president" to form special task forces. The purpose of this committee was to investigate, what in his opinion was, my careless handling of the community's finances and violation of bylaws. My bashing started again and Zeeshan and his accomplices reveled in their perceived power for the next three days. On June 30, their terms came to an end. Our new EC was advised to stay put for the next three days and dissolve the ad hoc committee by deferring action to the grievance committee during our first meeting. This was how it was done.

It took me a long time to reconcile with what I considered inaction of the grievance committee as well as community stakeholders. As my wounds healed, through professional and friendly counseling, I came to terms with many people. I had blamed some for acting as conspirators in the garb of mediators and a few others for claiming to be my guardians while giving defaulters a way out. Through reflection and conversations, I realized that most of them were good people with the best of intentions. Some were protecting me from a man of unpredictable nature while others were genuinely driven by the altruistic motive of keeping a small community intact.

Despite a year full of shocks and jolts, I was excited to start my year as the President of MAP on July 1, 2017. I had the best team to make it a fulfilling journey. We were all ready for a fresh start, to sincerely serve the house of *Allah* with dedication, and usher in a new era where social politics would have no room.

. 7 .

MADAM PRESIDENT

"You will be defined not just by what you achieve, but by what you survive."

- Sheryl Sandburg, COO Facebook

MAP required a lot of emotional as well as physical cleanup and our team set to work right away. Though there were some remnants of the last EC, all new officers were full of zest for doing the best. Before we embarked on our year of service, members of the EC, governing board and Sunday school administration had decided to seek professional help with a leadership mentor. During the prior tumultuous year, it was realized that most team members were well-intentioned but had little professional experience when it came to nonprofit management and leadership responsibilities. Those of us who had been a part of the last EC were fatigued by long, inconclusive meetings, which would deviate every second from the loosely set agenda. There was a need for professional guidance and support of organizational leadership at MAP. Through my connections at GSPIA, we were able to seek mentorship of Dr. Kevin Kearns, a professor and leadership development professional at the University of Pittsburgh.

During our first EC meeting, we laid down the foundation and vision for each of the education, social, outreach and facilities committees for the year. We discussed the much-needed technology updates, mosque security, communication policy and its privacy. With one of the *Eids* right around the corner, we started making arrangements for the holiday festival right away. And we cleared away the past baggage by deferring any standing grievances to be addressed where they belonged, that was, to our grievance committee.

I had felt bullied, emotionally and verbally harassed by men in the past EC. My male colleagues on the Executive Council 2017-18 restored my faith in the kindness of men and their original roles in our religion as support and protectors of women. Our president-elect, Omar Abbasi, especially took the brunt of many things while standing by me. Zeeshan and his supporters on the governing board tried to loop in our new EC members and cast doubts about my character and project management in the beginning, but my team chose to do the right thing instead of male bonding. They decided to not feed into gossip and past grievances, stay positive and forward focused. Together, we all made an invincible team and had all bases of our community covered across genders and demographics.

Dr. Kearns helped us harness our energies and channel them in the right direction. From conversations on nonprofit 101 and punctual meetings to the importance of an efficient board and strategic planning, Kearns helped us come to a common table and open a refreshing dialogue. We tried new things like consent agendas and timed meetings. One element that Kearns emphasized and has stayed with me since then is the value of empathy in an organization and among colleagues. Kearns' keen eyes and years of professional experience could readily decipher that part of our problems at MAP was intergenerational and cultural conflict. "The young are always about changing the system. Your new executive director comes in and says let's change these outdated bylaws. Well, guess what? Someone else says, they look perfectly fine to me; I actually wrote these by-laws! And then there is a conflict without any resolution." As Kearns walked through his presentation I could see myself having that conversation with Masood Haq. My self-reflection made me humble and more empathetic. It made me comfortable in my own skin and place, and not trying to win over anyone else. More than anything, it helped me reclaim my confidence and serve my community from my own perspective and gravity, rather than trying to outdo men and fit into any other shoes.

In addition to sessions with Dr. Kearns, I also personally attended leadership training sessions specifically those designed for faith-based leaders. I became an avid consumer of literature on effective church leadership. I developed a small network of friends who were leaders of their respective congregations in the Pittsburgh area. They helped me navigate rough waters with their advice and shared vision. If anything, they affirmed that we were all children of Adam, with fragile egos and petty rivalries across religions and cultures. It all provided a much-needed professional direction of turning me into a mosque President.

There were others outside of the MAP community who helped and provided guidance on many things that our young mosque was struggling with. Brad Orsini, who served as the Security Director for the Jewish Federation of Pittsburgh, helped us start the scary but important security conversations about having mechanisms in place for protecting our congregation. Pastor Dan Turney, of MAP's neighboring Christian Community Church (CCC) became my source for biblical information and congregational leadership. I enjoyed many enlightening talks with him. Our friends at other area mosques, Wasi Mohamed, Julie Webb and Elaine Linn at the Islamic Center of Pittsburgh and the leadership of the MCCGP, all provided help and support whenever I reached out to them. The Islamic Center of Pittsburgh especially became our close ally and we constantly shared ideas about breaking the silos both internally within the Muslim community as well as the greater Pittsburgh community.

Professionals and professional development did not do much to heal my personal scars. My past experiences had made me wary of men and my unconscious venom could only be unleashed on the only man in my life who would take it; the man who had been my husband for fifteen years by then. I was always in a bad mood, at the edge of my nerves, carrying the burden of feeling exploited by simple acts of life like getting out of bed in the morning. I outwardly looked confident but was internally depressed and becoming more so. I would lash out all the time at my family and sometimes cried in the quiet. My realization came when I got agitated with my mother in Pakistan during a simple phone conversation. She was distraught and so was I. At a time, when everyone complimented me on how well I was doing, I was secretly getting crushed under my own hidden trauma.

After long conversations with Bilal, I finally embraced the idea of professional counseling. I felt emotionally bruised and talking about what I had gone through brought me healing in an unanticipated way. Many things came out during the counseling session which was more like a venting avenue for my pent-up feelings. I was haunted by demons I was not even aware of. I recognized how I felt hurt, more by people I used to consider friends, than by the actions of those who looked seemingly responsible. I had signed up in the spirit of service, to God and my people and felt that I had suffered for it. I cried my heart out during the session. I cried at the injustice of social norms and mourned the loss of sanity from my life during this process. My therapist mostly listened quietly and gave me the much- needed outlet for my welled up grief. I did not have to go back to her after that first session. It looked like I just needed a shoulder to cry on and was mentally up and running after it.

Something beautiful happened after I confronted the unconscious demons of my life in their face. All the darkness that had started to pollute my soul was gone. I felt free and pure. The negativity of emotions left me, and it was almost as if I had started a new chapter in my personal life. I became more internally connected and spiritually religious. On most days, I would read the Quran to stay focused not only on a higher moral presence but also on my mission and purpose of serving the mosque. I found peace in what inspired me, that was, writing, teaching, learning and serving. I was invited to join the board of Northside Common Ministries (NCM), which housed the largest food pantry of Pittsburgh. I regained my calling in serving humanity through NCM. I made a commitment to myself to exercise regularly, eat mindfully and sit down with my family despite how busy the day might be. I disengaged myself mentally and spiritually from the people and events around myself. The flipside of it was that with eight months still remaining in the completion of my presidential tenure, I started feeling more like a critic of institutionalized religion than the head of a congregation.

After this emotional liberation, I actually started enjoying my time at MAP. I was amused at the situations and people that previously used to provoke and make me anxious and angry. This was the stuff sitcoms were made of. Or maybe it was more like a soap opera with tales of mixed loyalties, jealousy and intrigue. It was unbelievable to see what led to World War II come into play at this tiny mosque in rural PA. There were hardcore alliances as well as loosely held factions. A system of patronage was rooted in the *masjid- culture* from the governing board to the Sunday school. The kingmakers played most of us around like the pawns of chess. An individual or family would go up or down in graces as these stakeholders patronized, or lifted their blessings from a person. These promotions and demotions were based on how many parties a person hosted, and who was invited or seen there. This was the *Desi* version of kissing ass. An influential and well-liked family hosted the best parties, lived in a big house and drove the best cars. By 2017, we had already seen the rise and fall of our own organically grown Hitler.

Some blasts from the past continued to haunt us. Masood Haq's unnerving criticism pushed us to do our best. Omar and I would review and cover all angles of any issue, prepared to answer any obscure real or made-up questions. Our logistical nightmares, with limited staff and increasing congregants continued to be overwhelming. For the entire year, we explored cost-effective options for the additional plumbing and sewage for the building, which was going to be a literal manifestation of throwing money down the drain.

Like all good times, my term went by fast, maneuvering and juggling many firsts for MAP. We hosted the first *Nikah* ceremony and a funeral service in the same year, reminding us all of the passage of life. MAP allowed us a place to come together as a community in joy and sorrow. However, the most important time at the American mosques is the month-long celebration of Ramadan, which overlapped May and June, 2018, towards the end of our EC's term. Like past years, our EC also had some exciting plans for *Ramadan* at MAP that year. We made all arrangements with frugality and sustainability as foremost considerations.

Ramadan is the ninth of the twelve months of the Islamic calendar. The Islamic calendar follows lunar dates and therefore *Ramadan* falls every year on a different date. Roughly, each year the lunar calendar moves back ten days on the solar calendar. The month of *Ramadan*, involves twenty-nine or thirty days of fasting, ending with the sighting of the new moon for the month of *Shawwal*. The holiday of *Eid al-Fitr,* that marks the end of fasting, is celebrated on the first day of Shawwal. All healthy adult Muslims are required to fast from sunrise to sundown and allowed to eat during the time in-between.

Thanks to a growing interest in Islam, the recent presence of American Muslims in journalism and mosque outreach committees, many Americans of faiths other than Islam are now aware of what *Ramadan* is all about. Muslims have come to be identified as people who can go with limited eating, drinking and sex for thirty straight days. But, what most of the Americans do not know is that for our *ummah*, the essence of Ramadan is not fasting. It is actually eating. For Muslims, *Ramadan* means one long month of meal preparation and celebration of gluttony. We love making the most of our eating time. Just like the Christian tradition of lent has come to be defined by fish fries, *Ramadan* reminds one of *samosas* and *pakoras* rather than abstaining from food. In Muslim countries, there are lavish *sahur* and *iftar* buffets, to celebrate the "spirit" of Ramadan. American mosques, over the years, have developed their own *Ramadan* culture.

There are special nightly prayers during the thirty days of Ramadan called *taraweeh*. Performing *taraweeh* prayers during Ramadan is not mandatory for Muslims but is considered as an opportunity to spend more time remembering Allah during this holy month. These prayers also provide another good opportunity for the community to socialize. A *Hafiz*, a person who could verbatim recite all thirty books of the Quran, leads *taraweeh* prayers. During the first four years of MAP's inception, a *Hafiz* was temporarily hired during Ramadan to lead the *taraweeh* prayers. There were also times when volunteers had led prayers. By Ramadan 2018, we had a resident *imam* at MAP who was also a *Hafiz* and executed all religious responsibilities.

During the first few years of MAP's creation, *Ramadan* used to fall during the summer break. One of the earlier ECs decided to host *iftar* dinners, that is the breaking of fast, at the masjid for all thirty days. It was convenient, especially for children and stay-at-home mothers, since schools would be closed. They could sleep off the day while fasting and then arrive at the mosque in the evening for *iftar*. There was no need to cook or find alternatives to keeping kids busy. What could be better for kids than spending their evenings going into late nights in the devout company at the mosque. Our small community at that time, of no more than hundred people, could fit snugly into the rented office building that functioned as MAP during the earlier days of the mosque's creation.

As the MAP community grew, running the logistics of *Ramadan* became increasingly difficult. At any given *iftar* there could be anywhere from thirty to three hundred people. There was no way to anticipate the number of people on a particular night to make food arrangements. We used social media, sent out email reminders to encourage people to confirm attendance for particular iftars to the extent of personally contacting and cold calling on community members. Eventually, the administration became used to randomly ordering food, based on the idea of expected rather than actual numbers. Our social committee would use instincts and grapevine, to pry if there were any private parties happening on a particular night. Truckloads of plastic water bottles were bought to use during *iftar* and *taraweeh* prayers. Not only was it hard to stock this massive number of water bottles, they were ultimately wasted. The kids had water fights with them while their parents fulfilled their religious obligations. In order to create some social responsibility, we had purchased recycle bins with special covers to allow water bottles only, but mostly it was garbage that ended up in those bins.

Until I was part of the administration, I had not realized what it took to organize *Ramadan* at the mosque. During my days of growing up in Pakistan, there were no *Ramadan* celebrations at the area mosques. It was not even called *Ramadan* but *Ramzan* and was more like a month-long entertaining and eating fiesta, with our *sehri* and *iftar* buffets. One thing that I particularly remembered from my childhood, apart from hopping from one place to another for iftar parties, were true displays of generosity. In my native city, Karachi, curbsides would be lined up with plates of dates, traditional foods and water at iftar time, not only for those who could not afford a decent meal after a day of fasting but also for those who could not make it home for the meal in time. Since my family was not big on taraweeh prayers, most of our after- *iftar* activities involved going shopping or trip to the tailor, who needed constant reminders to turn in our newly stitched clothes by *chand raat* or night of the moon-sighting for *Eid*, to be adorned on the *Eid* day. *Ramadan* weekends were fun times , when we would pull an all-nighter of movie marathons, leading up to the predawn *sehri* meal.

Ramadan was taken to a whole different level by American Muslims. Nowhere was the "spirit of Ramadan" more evident than at smaller *masajids* like MAP, which had embraced *Ramadan* not only as a month of fast-track community building along with serious *sawab*-grabbing, but also hosted all the major events, from the Annual Fundraiser to the flagship interfaith event during this month.

Ramadan planning at MAP, therefore, involved intricate details from preparing and organizing two meals within 30 minutes of each other, of *iftar* and dinner for 30 days, haunting community to sign up and pledge for those meals, opening the mosque early in the evening and then closing late into night which sometimes meant after midnight. In-between all this, the cleaning had to be done and massive amounts of garbage had to be disposed. Additional serving and cleaning crew was hired to help around the mosque during *Ramadan* , as Muslims could not be bothered with anything except replenishing their body and spirits at this time with food, water and prayers. Extra days had to be arranged for garbage pickup much to the dismay of the garbage disposal company. There would be times when the garbage disposal company would forget to show up on the additional days and our *iftar* morsels also benefited the wildlife of Southwestern Pa.

Though many of my friends who grew up in Pakistan had adapted to the ease of spending their evenings at MAP during *Ramadan*, personally I could never get accustomed to this very American tradition. By the time I served as MAP's top administrator, every single day of Ramadan was during the school year. In response to a request from our EC to help close the mosque after *taraweeh*, a majority of community members expressed uncertainty about spending weekdays at MAP and therefore unable to help. Keeping that in mind and the consideration for saving food and utility wastage, we decided not to hold iftar dinners every day, but only three days over the weekend. MAP's social committee that took the brunt of Ramadan planning looked relieved at this decision and I busied myself working out arrangements for closing the mosque after midnight for thirty days.

The decision to not hold 30 *iftars* led to a small mutiny. It did not sit well with many people, especially those who had created "the legacy" of daily *iftars*. They could not let my legacy evolve by undoing their own. They petitioned the EC with many signatures and names of unlikely people, some of whom barely set foot in the mosque during *Ramadan*. Many others, who advocated for everyday Iftars, were the ones who had already declined to help with closing the mosque after *taraweeh*, because of their inability to attend during weekdays. People ganged up against the EC and it seemed as if we, the EC members, were standing between people and their way to God. It was high drama, social politics at its best.

As our then president-elect Omar and I circled some of our friends whose names appeared on the email petition, it looked like many infrequent mosque attendees were looped in on the precinct of providing meals for students and underserved Muslims, a community that was nonexistent in the suburbia, and hence was nowhere to be seen at MAP. Some characters who had tried to spread misunderstandings were quickly exposed by a few phone calls. We put together a calculated response, after multiple reviews by Omar, me and our spouses. It was cut-and-dry, communicating EC's reasoning in arriving at the decision for not hosting the daily Iftars at MAP, while expressing our ultimate willingness in not being an intruder between men and their path to God.

This, however, was only the beginning to our *Ramadan* woes. The next were the water wars. The long days of fasting during summer left little time to replenish the body's hydration needs. For the ease of those who are praying *taraweeh* late into night, earlier MAP administrations had provided some plastic water bottles so people could carry them in the praying area and keep with them. However, as the congregation grew so did the number of water bottles that would be required for everyone who performed *tarawih*. This multiplied our trash as well as carbon footprint and ours was not the only mosque administration concerned about this waste.

Islam had originated in the desert of Arabia. Many of Prophet

Muhammad's earlier followers were the underserved or those who left their families' riches and followed him. Those devout Muslims of the earlier years of Islam would fast not only during Ramadan, but even on other random days, as a way of leading an ascetic life. Such a practice to deny food and water to oneself is similar across Abrahamic and other faiths. In order to provide for those in need, there is a great emphasis in *Quran* and *Hadith* on supplying water for those who are fasting.

No one has taken this decree of providing water for the believers who are fasting more seriously than the American Muslims. Those at the Muslim Association of Greater Pittsburgh followed it to the letter. It started with one person picking up a truckload of water bottles from Costco, with money provided through community donations. The idea caught like wildfire. By Ramadan 2017, the mosque would be littered with plastic water bottles all over the internal and external premises of MAP. They filled up the ground dug for the proposed septic tank, creating a semblance of our own landfill. All appeals for putting the plastic in recycle bins fell on deaf ears.

Many national faith-based organizations and Pittsburgh-area congregations had committed to green initiatives, which included no plastic policy, as part of a life led through faith. Inspired by their respective scriptures, they found calling in mankind's role as stewards of earth and therefore responsible in protecting the earth granted to us. In order to align MAP with the mainstream cause of environmental protection, as well as out of our selfish worldly desire to reduce garbage pickup expenses, our EC decided not to provide plastic water bottles during Ramadan. Earlier during the year, we had handed out refill water bottles with MAP logo as a token of appreciation for mosque volunteers, who had comprised at least 70 percent of our community's population. Those bottles were now part of our green initiative campaign. It was inspired by the Islamic Society of North America's (ISNA) campaign "Greening our Ramadan." We encouraged our congregants to bring their MAP water bottles to the mosque and use them to refill water from the water coolers. We purchased extra coolers to be placed at many convenient locations inside the mosque. Many community members who had already started asking about contributing towards plastic water bottles were informed that those would not be needed. We felt proud of ourselves for accomplishing this task so conveniently.

Little did I know that what I considered compliance was actually denial. No one took our appeal seriously. A week before Ramadan, water bottles started arriving and filling up MAP hallways. They came in mysteriously, sometimes after Friday prayers, or during wee hours of the night. When I found out, my first instinct was to donate them to a local food pantry but my wise advisors on the EC held me in check. Instead, we just removed them to MAP's storage room in the basement. We identified the individuals who were bringing in these bottles and I personally talked to them. Though unabashed and defensive of their actions, it did deter further supply, at least for that year. Other community members who supported environmental efforts, lined up with me. They spoke during daily lecture times or *halaqas* and personally spread the word. Those who initially condemned EC for not providing basic necessities like disposable plastic water bottles, may not have had a change of heart but understood our reasoning. By the end of Ramadan 2018, to be seen around MAP with a plastic water bottle was quite a taboo. Our green campaign had a troubled start, but was eventually successful.

At that time, I often thought about the Jewish community's separation of the orthodox, conservative and reformist synagogues. It would be convenient to ascribe people with differing degrees of "religiosity" to separate congregations. Our humble premises, that brought Muslims of all colors, shapes and sizes in close proximity to each other, came with attached costs.

The days of Ramadan were one such cost we had to pay!

Several hiccups marked the first few days of Ramadan. The feeble infrastructure of our mosque's premises started to crumble under daily usage. The troubled sewage system began to collapse and there was water flowing from some mysterious source into the basement area that was used as a social gathering hall. As hungry and thirsty community members congregated at the mosque, day after day, frustrations ran rampant and as always, manifested themselves in bickering, gossip, and tense encounters.

In *Ramadan* 2018, I developed a habit of checking my email and social media pages as soon as I opened my eyes in bed. There would always be an email from a community well-wisher, informing me about some calamity from the previous night. Before I started my day, I would brace myself to address the situation.

It was one such day, at 3:30 a.m. in the morning as I got up for *sahur*, to commence my day of fasting. There had been an argument between a community member and our *Imam*. It was no ordinary community member. He served on the Imam Oversight Committee, which meant that technically, the *Imam* reported to him. He also served as an unofficial but de facto leader of the conservative segment of our congregation. The *Imam* had publicly chided him for being lax and on his cell phone during the *taraweeh* prayers and late night reflections.

The argument took a personal and ugly turn as half of the community tried to resolve the argument past midnight. I was not present, nor did anyone try to contact me. In the dead of the night, many people tried to arbitrate and made things worse between the aggrieved parties. By the time, the news reached me things were already out-of-hands, with tempers off the roof. I mumbled and grumbled, and eventually someone thought to involve me, the chief of the organization, at a point when the conversation had turned ugly to the point of no return. Given the popular opinion, we once again deferred action to Mr. Haq and a resolution was reached that left everyone feeling disenfranchised.

During that Ramadan, I felt many times that I was a mere peg in the greater scheme of things. A young woman like me did not belong at the table where decisions were made. My gender and age were always considered synonymous with inexperience and I was often cast out by the same people who had elected me to serve as the head of this congregation.

At most mosques across the United States, Annual Day of Giving or *Ramadan* Fundraiser is an important event. As people, we love a good bargain and nowhere is it more apparent than in our dealings with *Allah*. We love haggling, getting two or more for the price of one. For similar reasons we love doing charity and as promised by *Allah*, the best charity is the one practiced during Ramadan. According to one saying by the Prophet Muhammad, "*Allah* multiplies reward for charity during *Ramadan*, seventy times more than at any other time."

Ramadan in the United States was therefore fraught with fundraisers for all different kinds of causes and charities. Inspired by the black-tie fundraisers in America, where the rich, elite and corporate guests gathered to have a good time while supporting a cause, Muslim organizations had similarly modeled their fundraisers, but without the rich, elite and corporate guests. Our challenges were numerous. The Muslim community in America existed in small pockets and it was not easy to keep on raising funds over and again with the same people. Our event organizers, another fancy name for some unpaid volunteers, always had three big decisions to make.

1- The event budget was always tight. There would be debates amongst the organizers on the venue of the event, with the more frugal ones always presenting the possibility to hold the fundraiser at an area mosque and save expenses. Having a fundraiser at the mosque also eliminated the need for renting several rooms, which included a childcare area and separate area for performing *salah*. The thrifty group was almost always met with resistance by other organizers who believed that the best venue for a fundraiser was a four or five-star hotel or a grand ballroom. The compromise was often a two to three-star hotel, with ample lobby space for children to run around.

2- The second challenge, but probably more important than the first, was the food that would be served at the fundraiser. The organizers would spend a few months arguing if the best option for a meat dish were kebabs or goat curry, and between *samosa* and *pakora* which one would make a better appetizer. The choice of food also determined the choice of menu as not all hotels allowed third party catering.

3- There was always some entertainment needed at the fundraising event. Like food, the entertainment part of the program had to be kept *halal* as well. Music, for most gatherings , especially related to *masjid,* was not considered 100% halal. Our folks enjoyed a good laugh, but bathroom and sex jokes were not appreciated. A group of Muslim comedians by the name of "Allah Made Me Funny" provided entertainment at many Muslim fundraising events. Eventually, they were overused and had to be reminded at the time of the invitational contract of the year and event they had previously entertained the community that they were going to amuse again. Given this lack of options, a breed of speakers had emerged who merged humor and social issues while encouraging people to give at the same time. They had enough working knowledge of Islam to provide inspirational quotations from *Quran* and *Sunnah* and a huge

Twitter following that had turned them into household names.

Despite such meticulousness and efforts on part of our organizers to cater to varying preferences of community members, it was exceptionally hard to raise funds in the Pittsburgh-area given the small size of the Muslim community and the higher density of mosques. Not only that, many other humanitarian and social causes, including some from out-of-town, wanted to tap into the *masjid-crowd*. The masjid administrations would try to provide a balance in *Ramadan*, in satiating some believers' innate desire to give during the month, while addressing those of many others who complained that someone seemed to be raising funds for some great cause every time they were at the *masjid* during *Ramadan*.

However, in the interest of tradition and having enough to get by during the year, almost every mosque in the United States held its Annual Day of Giving during the month of *Ramadan*. They knew their clientele well and out of desperation, played with their emotions that encouraged them to give more! In the absence of any tithe, no concept of mandatory giving to *masjid* and ridiculously low membership fee, MAP could barely meet its operational expenses, let alone enhance programming. Since nothing defined giving in the way of Allah like contributing towards the house of Allah, MAP's biggest fundraiser was always during Ramadan when the spirituality and generosity of our community was at its peak.

If the *Ramadan* Fundraiser in 2017 was marked by ambivalence, the one to be held on June 3, 2018, was full of excitement and anticipation. A few minor skirmishes during the holy month were disregarded in the face of the greater good. This time around, the community's morale was high. For the first time, we were expecting to see some of our friends of other faiths at our fundraiser. And everyone enthusiastically waited to hear from our keynote speaker, Wajahat Ali.

Our Fundraising Chair, Hamid Jafri, had landed Wajahat Ali through a personal connection. Ali was a New York Times contributor and an accomplished writer and public speaker. Some in our community argued that Ali is too big a celebrity for our humble mosque. Many others including myself saw this as an opportunity to match an ambitious goal of $100,000 in one night. Ali was a Muslim celebrity and people could not wait to hear from him. The event sold out fast and all looked good until emails from student advocacy groups from across Pennsylvania started pouring in my email inbox.

The first email came from Temple University in Philadelphia. They requested that we reconsider our decision to host Ali for reasons of his insensitivity to the cause of Palestine. Ali had recently attended the controversial Shalom Hartman Institute and published his views on the stalemate in the Middle East. In a feature opinion piece "A Muslim Among Israeli Settlers" published by the Atlantic in June 2018, Ali had advocated for a "one-state solution" for Israel-Palestine dichotomy, which contradicted the wishes and views of majority of the leading American Muslim organizations.

In an objective universe, the Israel-Palestine issue would belong to the realm of International Affairs and not religion. It, however, has evolved as a religious contention for Muslims and Jews across the globe. Nowhere are religious connotations of this cause outside of the Middle East are more apparent than in the United States of America. Muslim leadership organizations, student advocacy groups and anyone else claiming to speak on behalf of Muslims likes to keep the cause of Palestine at the core of their mission.

As Wajahat Ali's views became public, the Islamic Society of North America (ISNA) disinvited him from the speaker's slate for their national conference. Another leading Muslim group, the Council on American Islamic Relations (CAIR) stood by ISNA in their stance. Ali rebutted in another op-ed published by The Atlantic, titled "I Talked to Zionists- Then I was Disinvited by a Major Muslim Group." After that, he took to Twitter to further his mission.

Ali's intention might be to use his legendary flippancy and give the situation a comic turn but the larger Muslim community identified his remarks as no less than blasphemy. For most, among his many other crimes, he had used the name of *Allah* to concoct bathroom humor, in a tweet; "I've said Allahu Akbar after taking giant dumps." Now, Ali had truly become too big for our small mosque. Going ahead with a speaker who had such claims to his credit was no different than serving Champagne at a Muslim fundraising event.

As the MAP Fundraising Committee exhaustively deliberated, letters started pouring in from a wide variety of audience asking us to disinvite Wajahat Ali. On Friday June 1, two days before our biggest fundraising event of the year, the Fundraising Committee decided to let Ali know that we could not host him to speak at our fundraiser. Ali claimed half of what he was promised in remuneration and we parted ways.

The bigger task, however, laid before us. Next, we had to deal with many of Ali's enthusiasts who were attending the event to come see and hear him speak. Another set of letters and social media comments started pouring in from the liberal sections of our community, with criticism directed at us in the name of free speech.

A lot of correspondence and conversations personally targeted me of hypocrisy and my reputation as a hard core liberal. Some of my closest friends were also disillusioned by our decision. In the microcosm of the Muslim community, there is an increasing sentiment of manipulation by the big national organizations in local spheres. Many at MAP felt that our segment of society, and a mosque like ours, should have disregarded ISNA and stood by Ali through such tough times for him.

Amidst the controversy that ensued, I strengthened myself for two days. I braced for questions and responded politely but candidly. I had to repeatedly explain the difference between my private and organizational preferences. We arrived at many decisions at our mosque, in the light of ISNA's rulings and guidance. We used ISNA's practice of astronomical moonsighting to announce our holidays. We had referred to them while making space for female leadership at our mosque, leading our green initiative and doing outreach while aligning ourselves with other faith-based organizations. However, what most people had not realized until that point was that deferring from ISNA was only one of our team's concerns. Our main preoccupation were emails from local student groups which requested/demanded disinviting Wajahat Ali, and our team was neither ready nor equipped to handle a protest outside the Marriott if these student groups showed up.

Miraculously, the evening of our annual fundraiser on June 3, 2018, was a beautiful and successful one. More than two hundred Pittsburgh-area Muslims came together in the Cranberry Marriott Ballroom and once again, raised over $100,000 for MAP in a single night. As we broke fast, prayed and laughed together, no one present in that room seemed to mind that our inspiration to give that night did not come from Wajahat Ali but instead from our dear friend and community member Omar Khawaja, as he held everyone hostage until the desired funds were raised. I was overwhelmed with gratitude.

The fundraiser was held towards the end of Ramadan and with only a few days remaining in my tenure as president. My community had made me immensely proud that night. These people had made me laugh and cry. We had ardently loved and vehemently argued with each other.

In the end, I was amazed at the vibrant energy of this small group of no more than three hundred families in Western Pennsylvania. They had great resilience, and unique courage, that was absolutely needed to call and practice their faith unabashedly and unapologetically, in today's America.

These were my people and I would be forever indebted to them for some memorable times.

. 8 .

FRIENDS FOREVER

"Girl," he said. "I just came to remind you, you don't have to carry this load all by yourself. To know that people care about how you're doing when the doing isn't so good- that's what love is. I feel blessed to know this for sure."

Oprah Winfrey, *What I Know for Sure*

It would be amiss if I take full credit for sailing smoothly through the journey of life, especially my years at MAP, all by myself. At every stage, I was blessed to have friends, whom I could rely on for help and support. Some of these were the people who had never set foot in a *masjid* before but showed up on election days and fundraisers in my support. Some others could have found an easy way out, on the pretext of diplomacy like many others, but instead chose to stand openly by my side. Yet, others were not even Muslims, but were always there to help, advise and listen. These were my people, and such was my tribe.

I have never been the one to show affection or display heartfelt emotions. This has hindered my ability not only to have many friends but also to retain them. Top it with my workaholic nature and an obsessive compulsion to productively fill every second of my time , and you would know the reason for my lifelong dilemma of trying hard to find and then easily losing touch with those friends. However, despite my solitary nature, I was never without friends while growing up. I still have friends from grade school, who are now more like social media friends, but we never miss an opportunity to "Like" or "Love" each other's posts. I have recently reconnected with old friends in Pakistan through WhatsApp, and though our conversations have changed from musings and aspirations to hardcore facts of life, our bond remains the same.

In my days of youth, I used to joke that I was an acquired taste. I could not appease everyone, nor did I make any effort to do so. My upbringing in a large close-knit family, with grandparents, uncles, aunts and cousins, in addition to my parents and brothers, never allowed for the solitude that would make friendships outside of the family necessary. I never needed or had to seek out more people in my life.

Immigration changed my existence. For the first time, I found myself in need of people. From advice on making a country home and taking care of a baby to leadership conversations on effectively running an organization, I had to invest time and energy in constant search of people who had been there before me, or were simply there for me. In the circus of *Desi* herd parties, these folks provided an oasis of calm friendship. During our 15 years of living in Pittsburgh, Bilal and I came to call a variety of people our friends. Our bubble would grow and shrink from time to time, but these folks were at the core, and always remained the same. We could call upon them during joy and sorrow.

During my initial days in Pittsburgh, I searched for faces like mine, everywhere from malls to restaurants and grocery stores. The slightest whiff of the sound of *Urdu* or *Hindi* would hold my attention and send my gaze searching for the speaker.

I met many people, some of whom would go on to become great friends, at a picnic organized by the Islamic Center of Pittsburgh in 2004, during our first summer in Pittsburgh. At that picnic, most people simply stared inquisitively at me; a newbie to the Pittsburgh Muslim community at that time. I was too preoccupied with the feed-diaper change-nap cycle of my baby, who was a couple of months at that time, to engage with anyone in a conversation. Still, somewhere over the cookout and watermelon, I found a lifelong friend in Rabia Khan. Our upbringing in Karachi, residence in the South Hills of Pittsburgh and the stuck-at-home situation, mine with a baby and hers with a toddler, gave us plenty to talk about. Eventually life would take us on different paths, with more children and moving to different parts of town. Rabia would go on to homeschool her third child, grow vegetables in her garden, harvest bees and sell honey. I would even forget to water the few annuals in my yard. Her husband, Shahab, was a hunter, while mine had once killed a bird under peer pressure, in his youth, and lived to regret it for the rest of his life. Our families still found enough to share around Rabia's amazing Deer *Nihari* and apple pie. To this day, my fourteen-year-old remains "Baby Girl" for this family.

There is no Pakistani food like *Nihari*. This is, perhaps, a personal bias but it is a bias that I refuse to shed. One of my major concerns in moving to Pittsburgh in the first place was its lack of Pakistani restaurants and hence a place to get good *Nihari*. The few Indian restaurants in Pittsburgh at that time did not offer traditional *Nihari* that is made with beef, as cow was a sacred animal for them. In the *Nihari* desert that Pittsburgh was, Lubna Rahman rescued me.

Lubna and her husband Pervaiz Rahman were my youngest uncle's friends from Karachi. The two men had known each other for five decades by the time I moved to Pittsburgh. My uncle connected me with the Rahmans while I was moving to Pittsburgh. One of the first questions I had asked Lubna Auntie before moving to Pittsburgh was about the best place to get *Nihari* from in the city. I am sure she could sense my disappointment at her answer, as the first time she showed up at my house once we moved to Pittsburgh, was with a large serving of homemade but professional quality *Nihari*. She even shared her recipe with me, which is a big favor in the *Desi* community where recipes are considered family secrets.

Over the years of living in Pittsburgh, the Rahmans would become surrogate parents for Bilal and myself. They were not a full generation older than us, but we started calling them uncle and auntie, because of the love and care they showed to us. We would often turn to them not only for career and professional advice but also social counseling. At the time when my first daughter was a newborn, and an entire community showered me with advice regarding the rights and wrongs of *Desi* motherhood, Lubna Auntie encouraged me to attend graduate school. Though we would not meet often, the Rahmans were there when we needed them, during holidays, child births and important occasions. They were never a part of the MAP community, but came out to support me at the fundraiser in 2017, at a time when I needed reassurance from my people.

When we were moving to Pittsburgh, someone once described the city to me as "naive but understanding." After fifteen years of living in Pittsburgh,

I would replace understanding with caring. Never was this care more evident, then after the presidential election of 2016. As the Trump presidency was announced, there were friends who showed up at my house to assure us of their support. Wexford, in the far north of Allegheny County, was a mostly Republican neighborhood. Some of our non-Muslim friends who were registered Republicans, voted otherwise during the election, to show their opposition for Trump's discriminatory policies. There were neighbors who went through the effort of figuring out our holidays and bringing us holiday gifts.

And then there were friends who were like family. If you are a Muslim in America, these are the people you would celebrate Halloween with.

For many Muslims, especially immigrants, Halloween is synonymous to devil worshipping. Some have dubbed it a celebration of *Shaitan's* birthday, in an effort to convince kids to stay away from the schools' costume parade and Halloween parties. Weeks before Halloween, mosques across America start showering kids with candy in the hope of saving them from the sins they might commit on October 31.

Some of us irredeemable souls still celebrated Halloween and did so with a bang! We got together in fun costumes and relished Chinese and Middle Eastern takeout after a mostly cold, rainy night of trick-o-treating with kids. Often, our family's partners-in-crime in pursuit of a halal Halloween celebration, were Sidra and Cyrus Khan. From our days of living together in the same townhouse community at Marshall Heights, we had seen each other through many good and bad times . Our children grew up together and were more siblings than friends.

The Marshall Heights community was a *Desi* paradise. Many South Asian families lived on the same street and shared a common backyard. *Ramadan, Eid, Holi* and *Diwali* were celebrated on the street.

Ruchi and Amit were our next-door neighbors. In Ruchi, I found a friend like no other. Originally from India, her intelligence, sincerity and good humor nullified many years of my Pakistan History classes from grade school to college, which always highlighted differences between Hindus and Muslims. Though not a Muslim herself, Ruchi hosted an *iftar* party for us, her Muslim friends, every *Ramadan*. She was the person my kids looked forward to meeting the most on *Eid* and receive *Eidi* from their Ruchi auntie.

As Muslims, our belief is that God never tests anyone beyond their abilities to bear the trauma. He would only give you the hardship that you could bear. The immigrant experience for the young would be a path of stones, if it was not for the care and cultural cultivation by those who have been here before us. Over the years, Bilal and I became close friends with a group of individuals who collectively went by the title of "Seniors" in the Muslim community of Pittsburgh. Some of them were even older than my parents, but we always enjoyed their warm exuberance and honesty that is often the gift of age. Naveed and Kazim Reza, Nighat and Hamid Ali, Shahnaz and Rizwan Mahmood and Azra and Arshad Mahmood , belonged to a generation that had moved to the United States before ours, led professional lives and raised children in this country , had seen them through education, marriages, in some cases divorces and then remarriages. Their presence brought light-hearted humor and fun during good times and perceptive insight during periods of dissonance.

Arshad Mahmood, in particular, became my support not only during the final tumultuous days of 2017, but all through my year of presidency in 2018. There were things during my tenure that I was able to achieve only because I knew he had my back. He came to "conflict resolution" meetings called by Zeeshan Ahmed and Masood Haq, so people like Yumna and me could not be bullied there. He was there to make sure that our contract for MAP's basement renovations goes through smoothly, without obstructions from those who wished otherwise.

I have to admit that initially, I failed to understand Arshad *bhai* and his motives. Now the President of the governing board, he was an influential community member during my years with MAP. There were times when I might have blamed him for inaction or diplomacy which seemed more like injustice. However, I later realized that Arshad *bhai* was one of the people who could see good in every person and situation. While most of us were reactionary, Arshad *bhai* was a visionary. A person like him was nowhere to be found in the Muslim community of Pittsburgh. He was one of the biggest, if not the largest, financial supporter of MAP, but was hardly seen at the mosque. With his two daughters raised and gone, Arshad Bhai and his wife Azra, who served as the Principal of MAP Sunday School for a long time, had adopted a third child in MAP.

"You will always be too much for some people. Those are not your people." I have seen these words float around on social media hundreds of times, as profile pics and statuses, but I truly appreciate whoever first wrote those words. There is wisdom in them. It is almost impossible to answer the question; "What makes a great friend?" There are different things that bring us close to different people. Sometimes, these people are as different from us as East is from the West, but therein lie the similarities: they are both a part of the same compass. We can play our distinct roles on the path of life, without judgment and threatening another's worldview.

I have not known anyone who understood that better than Navin and Sharjeel Farooq. They were among the few good friends I had, but their own social circle was big and diverse. From MAP to dance parties and nightclubs, these two could fit anywhere. You could talk to them about topics as varied as philosophy and cricket. A rare sight at MAP, before or after my tenure, I would always remember Navin and Sharjeel among friendly faces I could count on to see, as I addressed gatherings at the mosque.

Thanksgiving for our family meant dinner at Noorafshan and Burhan Mahmood's house in Pittsburgh. Though I remember the warmth of this close-knit dinner that they hosted year after year, I specifically remember Thanksgiving 2014, when another friend, Maliha, floated the idea to form The Book Club. Sometime after the meal of Turkey and *Biryani,* over a cup of *chai,* our Book Club was born.

The Book Club was a result of the necessity to have conversation about ideas and not people. It eventually defined friendship for those of us who became and remained a part of it. Reading and discussing books brought us so close to each other, that we started functioning like a secret society. Our mantra, "What happens at The Book Club, stays at The Book Club," created a safe zone for everyone involved. After some initial skirmishes and attempts at infiltration, we limited the number of The Book Club members and were extremely selective in who could be inducted into it. The result was a diverse group of *Desi* women, that included professionals, homemakers and new moms, who enjoyed each other's company and were bound together by their passion for reading.

Many times, Noorafshan, Maliha and I wished that Sara Abbas could be part of The Book Club. She was the most book-clubbiest person one could think of. But she had moved from Pittsburgh to New Jersey and later to West Virginia by the time our Book Club was born.

Like Rabia, I first met Sara at a mosque picnic as well. Unlike Rabia and myself, Sara and I did not click instantly. Sara had three very boyish boys and I had one very girly girl. She was a graduate student at the prestigious Carnegie Mellon University, while I was a haggard mother and housewife. After a few days, we met at a *Desi* party with so many people that there was hardly any space to move. In that chaos, I stepped on and crushed Sara's foot with my two-inch heels. Sara survived it. But for obvious reasons, I did not see her anywhere in my close proximity for a few years after that.

I am glad to say that I did not make a lasting impression on Sara during those first encounters. I am not sure how it all worked out eventually, but by 2013 Sara and I were good friends. By 2018, we were great friends. And by 2020, we would be the best of friends. Sara became one of the friends whom I could completely open my heart to. A few steps ahead of me in life, Sara could always steer me in the right direction. I seldom show my vulnerabilities to people, but in Sara I found a confidante. Sara's husband, Ghulam Abbas, also became a trusted advisor for Bilal, in matters of life and profession.

I feel privileged to call all these wonderful people my friends. But words escape me in talking about one person who, over the years, became more than a friend. Sabeen Iqbal, became the older sister that I never had. Bilal and I had known Sabeen and her husband Nadeem Iqbal for a long time, but I truly got to know her during my first year at MAP. To an outsider, Sabeen would be an epitome of grace, class and sincerity. But, for her friends she was much more than that. Over the years, she became my fiercest advocate and closest ally. A physician by education and homemaker by choice, her creativity and originality of ideas was unmatched. She provided true meaning to be a servant of God, through her devotion and service both to the creator and His creations. A selfless individual, there were times when Sabeen would be a caregiver for three individuals, her daughter who had Prader-Willi syndrome, and her elderly mother and mother-in-law. She never complained and always found time to look the best and do the best.

Sabeen and my friendship had gained strength during stormy days at MAP in 2017. We had worked together on the very controversial basement renovation project and counselled many decisions. Sabeen stood by me to bear the brunt and help me fight back accusations and slander. Never to claim limelight for herself, she grudgingly accepted to serve as the Education Secretary during my tenure as president, in addition to her position on the governing board. She took the MAP Education Committee to new heights, ensuring diversity of programming across gender, age and interests. Our friendship only grew stronger over the years and continues to do so.

While growing up in Pakistan, my parents kept a close eye on the crowd my brothers and I would hang out with. My mother would often say that we became the very people we surround ourselves with. She always reinforced the value of cultivating deep meaningful friendships, rather than plenty of fleeting ones. I feel fortunate that I had the opportunity to call many cities and two different countries home, meet people and grow with them. My friends have inspired me to be a better person, a better mother and a good friend in return.

. 9 .

ARRIVING

"When we strive to become better than we are, everything around us becomes better too."

-Paulo Coelho, Brazilian lyricist and novelist

It was somewhere around my tenth year of living in Pittsburgh that I started considering myself more of a Yinzer and less of a Karachiite. I felt shaped by the city and the unique opportunities it provided for my family and myself. Grad school and my limited but meaningful work with the Allegheny County DHS opened up Pittsburgh to me in unique ways.

"As years went by, I held onto Pittsburgh. And Pittsburgh held onto me, with its educational opportunities, affordability and growing diversity," I wrote in a first-person op-ed, "From Pakistan to Pittsburgh" published by the Pittsburgh Post-Gazette on March 5, 2016.

One could not claim to be a Pennsylvanian unless they pay homage to the resident weather prophet, Punxsutawney Phil. He was the official weatherman of Pennsylvania and was entitled to

Hollywood fame by virtue of "The Groundhog Day" movie named after him. Every Feb. 2, at 6 a.m., the sage of sages, prognosticator of prognosticators, came out of its abode at the Gobblers Knob in Punxsutawney, Pa., to give good tidings of spring or six more weeks of snow. The legend has it that if Phil sees his shadow, on this day, he would run back to his burrow, predicting six more weeks of winter. If he does not see his shadow, it was springtime, baby!

The tradition of animals predicting weather is rooted deep in many cultures around the world including those in South Asia. It came to America with German Settlers in the nineteenth century. Since the first Groundhog Day celebrated in Punxsutawney, Pa., in 1886, Mr. Phil has been predicting weather with the miracle of at least 50% accuracy. Every summer, he drinks the Elixir of Life that adds another seventy years to his immortality. It was folklore like Groundhog Day that made me interested in getting to know more about the region and take pride in my identity as a Southwestern Pennsylvanian.

Our family saw Phil make his prediction, year after year, through live video streaming. In 2018, we planned to make a pilgrimage to see "the prophet" in the flesh. However, we were deeply saddened to find that a couple of months in advance of the grand event on February 2, it was impossible to find a place not only in the holy town of Punxsutawney, but anywhere within fifty miles of it. In response to an opinion piece I published in the Pittsburgh Post-Gazette documenting our family's fascination with Phil and the universality of folklore, we received "the call" from Punxsy Town to be a guest of honor at the Groundhog Day ceremonies. The girls and I were overjoyed at the opportunity to be finally in the presence of the great sage, who was definitely more reliable than the weather channels.

On that very cold February 1, 2018, the girls and I drove down to Punxsutawney, eighty-four miles northeast of Pittsburgh. We passed Amish buggies and small towns to arrive just in time for the Members Special. The Groundhog Club had graciously arranged for our boarding as well as VIP tickets to all the special events over the weekend. We were ecstatic to meet Phil for the first time. There was a community banquet at night followed by the grand finale of all ceremonies, the actual Groundhog Day prediction, early in the morning. Amidst all the mirth and merriment around us, no one seemed to mind the news of six more weeks of winter. All the "Believers" were a happy bunch of people.

Our time in Punxsutawney, with all the festivities, were fun two days for our family but what I remembered most from that trip were people. They were the most genuine people I had ever met in my life. A.J. Derume of Groundhog Club's Inner Circle and Katie Donald, the Club's executive director, went above and beyond to make this a time to remember for our family. Our stay was arranged with a local family for a fully immersive experience and we had front of the line passes for the final event. Our gracious hosts, Dave Gigliotti "The Thunder Maker" for the Inner Circle, his wife Carla and their four children, opened their beautiful home to us. Carla and I found ourselves passionate about the same things, which included obsessing over our wardrobe to the Groundhog Day special events and discussing misplaced priorities of the American public school system. Carla was born and had lived in South Africa till the age of sixteen. She was one of the few people we came across who were familiar with the game of squash and the girls were excited to talk to her about the sport.

In the wake of the 2016 presidential elections, small towns in Pennsylvania were counted as the "Trump Country." It was considered that Muslims and people of color did not belong in such a place. I was both, according to my ethnicity and nationality. Many friends expressed concern to me about this, as I was preparing for my trip to Punxsutawney. As a native city dweller myself, I would confess to have harbored personal biases about denizens of small towns. Punxsutawney not only changed my views but also touched my heart, with its warmth, love and ingenuity.

My girls and I might be the only people of our color and ethnicity in the room at the Groundhog Day events, but not for a second did we feel unwelcome or insecure. This was a place where we were loved for our "otherness." Not only were we acknowledged at all the special events, A.J., our host made a point of detailing for everyone, similarities across cultures from Pakistan to Punxsutawney. A local family invited us to an open house brunch. As I laughed and talked with these friends I had made over the weekend, I could not help but marvel at how important it was for all Americans to meet and connect with each other at a personal level. We may be divided geographically across urban, suburban and rural, or politically into Republicans or Democrats, but we all can find joy in simple things our lives had to offer. We all loved some good old-fashioned fun and no other time offered it better than the Groundhog Day! Our trip to Punxsutawney made me embrace my cultural heritage as a Pakistani, and talk about it unabashedly, which Muslim outreach specialists advised against, in order to create an American Muslim narrative.

My trip to Punxsutawney took me back to my roots, exposing and placing me among people who were true to who they were and took pride in it. I yearned to stop functioning as an entity on documentaries and at interfaith tables. I wanted to share the intricacies, the beauty of my faith, the music and the arts, silly anecdotes and profound folklore to write my American Muslim story. I desired to change my narrative, which might not always include a struggle to find common ground but instead found unity in diversity. I increasingly desired that the American Muslims could branch out and let go images of stoic Muslim men and women who lined up for prayers all the time and kept daylong fasts. Trump's America had to be acquainted with the everyday Muslim and it was imperative for us, the American Muslims, to respond to our calling. It was time that America met the Muslim who worked the day job in its offices, coached the local soccer teams over the weekends and went to bed worrying about his mortgage and the upcoming college tuition for his oldest child. Sometimes he missed Friday prayers for a work commitment. On other times, because of a meeting at his children's school. This Muslim resided in every neighborhood, city and town. I desired to introduce that Muslim to America; the Muslim it had been familiar with for a long time but did not recognize as one of its own, but rather an "other." After the election of Donald Trump, many American Muslim writers, comedians and artists of my generation were working hard to streamline this recognition. At times, these Muslim ambassadors had done their outreach at the cost of alienating conservative factions of their own families and community.

I found my opportunity in teaching at the Osher Lifelong Learning Institute (OLLI) at the University of Pittsburgh. In Fall 2019, I was selected to teach a course "Muslims in the Neighborhood" to a class of approximately 50 students.

Osher Programs are based at American colleges and universities, and emerged out of a desire of their founder, the philanthropist Bernard Osher, to keep intellectual curiosity and a passion for lifelong learning alive for people aged fifty and better. The classes range from exploratory, to special interest and hands-on ones, covering a wide variety of topics including religion, arts, society and many others. In 2018, Sharon Gretz had newly joined the OLLI program at the University of Pittsburgh as Program Director. A major area of focus for her was to increase the diversity of the student body through deliberate efforts with minority communities. Not surprisingly, at least 90 percent of the OLLI members at the University of Pittsburgh in 2018 were white. There was some Jewish presence, and not more than a handful of Black students. There were no Muslim students at all, but the program had offered classes on Islam for several years, which were among some of the most attended at the Institute.

During my five classes for the course "Muslims in the Neighborhood," we explored various aspects of Muslim life and Islamic faith in America. We talked about what it meant to carry multiple identities, integration of Muslim faith with arts and architecture. We explored the diversity within the Muslim community and the fact that Muslims came in myriad of colors, ethnicities and temperaments. If I had a running theme for five classes, it was to leave my students with the notion that there was no one or perfect mold of a Muslim. The highlight of the course was a meet and greet with some Pittsburgh-area Muslims at the Islamic Center of Pittsburgh (ICP). I was deliberate and specific in my sample of Muslims. I included anyone who called him or herself a Muslim. I had arranged for my students to meet with women who covered their heads and some who did not, like myself. There were men who prayed five times a day, and others who even thought of Friday congregational prayers as a chore. It included Muslims by birth and some others by choice. Some of the attendees were born in the United States of America, others had become citizens through naturalization. A few there were still citizens of other countries, still navigating the impossibilities of the American immigration process after years of living here. Yet, we all came under one banner of American Muslims.

My intention in introducing my "Osher kids" to this sampling of

American Muslims was to spur them into looking around themselves for Muslims in their own neighborhoods and everyday lives. That would be the way to redemption in America, that was, to be recognized for who we were in essence. My students at OLLI were mostly retired and semiretired individuals. They included Pittsburghers from elderly homemakers to those who had finished distinguished careers. I might have been their teacher, but I was also the beneficiary of the wisdom that many of my students had accumulated over advancing years. They were well-traveled, knowledgeable and inquisitive. They had an unabashed capacity for argument and discourse, with each other as well as with me. I had to prepare well for the class, in order to be able to facilitate a robust debate.

Teaching a course on Islam in the twenty-first century America was like walking on a tight rope. I had no idea about the backgrounds of people who were attending my class. As a teacher, I would be considered a subject specialist and probably the best specimen of a Muslim that was around. This responsibility bore heavily on me. However, in the end I made a commitment to myself to stay honest and candid, while teaching and answering questions.

Despite the focus of the course on Muslims in America, international affairs continued to haunt our class from time to time. The Middle East kept on coming up. Saudi Arabia was also thrown around quite a bit. Our class discussions often started broaching into topics like acid attacks on women in Pakistan and the nuclear threat that Iran posed for the Western world. I had to consciously pepper my lectures with reminders that highlighted the uniqueness of American Muslim culture, rooted in American values of life, liberty and pursuit of happiness.

I had designed the course with a purpose to familiarize people with Muslims in America. But I quickly realized that it was not an easy task to erase the graphic images of turbaned Muslims committing atrocities in the name of my religion that were already etched on the hearts and minds of people. We waddled together and explored. Ultimately, my students turned out to be the most open-minded individuals, who dared to attend prayers at the Islamic Center of Pittsburgh at a time when many others thought of mosques as terrorist cells. In the end, we all taught each other a thing or two about our religions and ourselves. By the last class, I felt that I had vindicated my religion for at least this group of fifty individuals, in Pittsburgh.

Spending time in the company of Osher members inadvertently taught me many valuable lessons. I stopped fearing the passing of time and came to realize that every age was a stepping-stone in the journey of life. I felt less stuck in my life in the suburbia and the prospect of good schools that tied us to it. Many of my students had spent lives like mine, where the lackluster rut of life had eventually given way to travel and time to explore finer aspirations. I was inspired to be in the presence of so many epic voyagers, who continued to evolve and find new paths as the bullet train of life carried them along.

Fall 2018 was a formative time in my life. I felt engaged and accomplished at last. I had finished a successful year at MAP, earlier that spring. I was doing what I did best- writing, teaching and volunteering. I was also selected to attend the flagship program at Leadership Pittsburgh Inc.

If I have to define Leadership Pittsburgh in my own words, I would call it a crash course into Pittsburgh's history with a lens to the future. It prides itself as "the foremost multi-disciplinary leadership identification, enrichment and networking organization in Southwestern Pennsylvania dedicated to developing a robust pipeline of diverse civic leaders to serve the region." Through a ten-month program "participants get a deeper, behind-the-scenes understanding of the connected systems of the region, meet with the movers and shakers, view the community, its assets and opportunities in a new and profound way- and above all, get super-energized to increase their impact."

Leadership Pittsburgh might be a premium civic leadership program but I benefited from it more at a personal level by being in the presence of those who knew Pittsburgh in and out. My time at Leadership Pittsburgh helped me shape ideas into actions. It planted me amidst a group of sixty highly motivated civic and professional leaders who all came together around one cause with a singularity of focus, that was, to make Pittsburgh thrive.

My friends, Omar Khawaja, Ishfaq *bhai*, and Sharjeel, had all attended Leadership Pittsburgh at different points. Omar had helped develop a platform of stakeholders, that supported Muslim leadership of Pittsburgh to find a seat at the table, in order to network and further hone their leadership skills. They highly recommended the program to me and me to the program board. Initially, when it was proposed to me, I was not inclined towards it. Having felt the burn of so-called leadership at MAP, I did not even want to hear about any program that presented leadership almost as a vocation. I might have raised the bar to do my best and do justice to my role as the president of MAP, but, leadership to me had become a hollow word, a fancy name given to resolving petty disputes and attending a plethora of inconclusive meetings.

I had landed in Leadership Pittsburgh after spending thirteen years in Pittsburgh and thought that I knew the region well. It soon dawned on me that I was wrong. During my time with Leadership Pittsburgh, I came to be acquainted with another Pittsburgh that thrived or sometimes struggled to survive alongside my Pittsburgh. "Half of Pittsburgh remembers nothing of its past, while the other thinks about it far too much," Franklin Toker said in his book, *Pittsburgh: A New Portrait.* While many transplants to the region like myself were fighting to write our narrative in the story of Pittsburgh, many others were part of a battle to save their age-old story from erosion from these same pages.

Leadership Pittsburgh wanted these two Pittsburghs to become one and benefit from each other's stories of success and failure. Under the dynamic leadership and constant scrutiny of Aradhna Malhotra Oliphant, we sat together and travelled to distant parts of Pittsburgh, class after class, month after month.

Leadership Pittsburgh helped me break out of my comfort zone like no other experience. It was here that I truly learnt the American value of free speech. My classmates were doing great things, in corporate, civic, and non-profit worlds. They inspired me to greatness as well. I realized that I did not have to ever suck it up, unless I wanted to. This was my inspiration to become an advocate for anti-fracking movement in Southwestern Pennsylvania and ultimately, across America.

On a random day, in April 2019, I received an email through my neighborhood email distribution list that the Franklin Park Borough Council was getting ready to lease the State Game Land adjacent to I-79 to private interests for potential fracking. The proposed section of the game land was to fall in my neighborhood's backyard, not metaphorically but quite literally. Despite that, the email forwarded to our neighborhood was from another neighborhood and was exploratory in nature. People had heard things, but no one knew what was going on.

The email sprung many but not all of us who lived on Fox Chase

Drive, in 2019, into action. While some, like myself, started to dig through council meeting minutes, in an effort to find the whole truth, there were others who dismissed or simply did not care about it. News went around that one of the homeowners had already committed himself to a drilling interest, privately. There were conspiracy theories going around, about the borough council, different neighborhoods in the area, and our own neighbors as well. It also seemed that we, who lived on the Fox Chase Drive would be the most affected and least informed. The Borough had previously attempted to make deals with PennEnergy Resources, an oil and gas company, at their meeting during the holidays, anticipating not much community presence at that time. They might have been right about the suburbanites being busy with their holiday lights and planning meals at that time, but an environmentalist group, Food and Water Watch (FWW) got a whiff of the plans. FWW rallied up whoever they could at the short notice and showed up at the Borough Council meeting with almost hundred people and crew from local news channels. The borough council took refuge in not passing any motion in favor of fracking in the area at that time.

The matter was swept under the rug, but little known to the Borough Council was the fact that FWW was keeping a close tab on their activities. As soon as they saw an action item in the Council meeting's agenda for voting on fracking, they immediately alerted the residents of the affected area. FWW organized community meetings to better prepare the residents for advocacy. The first meeting I attended was on a Friday, the same as one of MAP's family nights and also the one when my parents-in-law were arriving from Pakistan. As I weighed my priorities as to where should I be spending time that night, I realized how far I have been indoctrinated into the American tradition of "not throwing away my shot." I went to the FWW meeting.

The following months ensued a long battle between the Franklin Park Borough Council and its residents. I personally experienced the Council President's backlash in response to a Letter to the Editor I published in the Pittsburgh Post-Gazette, detailing the Council's underhand approach and sidelining the taxpayers. After I spoke at the Council meeting in May, the President questioned me: "I read the letter that you have recently published. Are you suggesting that we ban fracking from Franklin Park?" I did not have to answer that question as an audience of over a hundred people in the room, responded with a resounding Yes!

During that inconclusive meeting, the Franklin Park Borough once again tabled the motion to decide on the layoff area for "commercial activity", and deferred it to another meeting. No such decision was made in near future. In the local elections of November 2019, the residents of Franklin Park voted out three members of a previously entirely Republican council. One of the new council members was Dr. Jiang Li, a first-generation immigrant and scientist who worked at the University of Pittsburgh. The impact of our efforts, as such, was way more than averting the danger of fracking from our area. It impacted the politics and power dynamics of Southwestern Pa.

While pursuing our fight for a common goal, I got to know my neighbors on Fox Chase in a way I could not do during six years of living on the street. Bilal and I were the only immigrants of all the residents on our block. We might have been unconsciously judged by others just as we had sometimes judged our neighbors when the yard signs went up during election seasons over the years. But fracking brought us together, especially the women of the neighborhood. We were a group of lawyers, doctors, writers and community organizers, who became a force to reckon with for the Borough Council. Belle Zimmer organized and updated the neighborhood, Elizabeth Cameron guided us all, Sylvia Choi spoke about health hazards, Rosemary O'Neill opened her home for community gatherings in addition to garnering area support, and I wrote, presented and took the word to Harrisburg as part of my Leadership Pittsburgh retreat in June. Many others joined and supported us, especially our beloved neighbor Eddie, a former Marine, who put the council members on a hot bed and kept them engaged for almost three quarters of an hour, far beyond his assigned time of five minutes and a restriction on asking questions. Fox Chase Drive had found camaraderie in very unusual circumstances.

I was now labelled officially as a social activist. I had two passions. The first, to make this world a better place for every human being and secondly, to make America a better country for all minorities and people of color.

I was a writer, guest speaker and panelist for events across Pittsburgh. In the following fall, I would be selected as an instructor for another class at OLLI, titled "Stronger than Hate: Building Inclusive Communities." The topic of the course reflected the city wide theme for Pittsburgh that year, after the horrific shooting at the Tree of Life synagogue in Pittsburgh's Squirrel Hill neighborhood, in 2018.

The shooting at The Tree of Life or L'Simcha synagogue has to be the most tragic event I had witnessed during my seventeen years in America. An armed person, who harbored anti-Semitic and anti-immigrant sentiments, entered synagogue during Shabbat services, on Saturday, October 27, 2018 and opened fire. He killed eleven innocent people and some of the families impacted included my students from the Osher Institute.

The shooting sprung the Pittsburgh interfaith community to action. In a dynamic effort initially set up by two national Muslim organizations but locally led by Wasi Mohamed, executive director of the Islamic Center of Pittsburgh at the time, Muslims of Pittsburgh and then from around the world contributed an over of $200,00 to support the grieving families and the impacted synagogue in whatever way it was needed.

The Tree of Life incident had resonated with the Muslim community of America at a personal level. One of my friends, Fayiza Mudassar, put it best, while recounting an incident at MAP in 2016, when a motorcyclist zoomed by the mosque hurling slurs like: "Go home!" In an open gun culture, it could have meant more than verbal abuse. "He could just, you know, open fire," Fayiza said when I interviewed her for an investigative report regarding the security climate for places of worship.

In this landscape, it was important for all the minorities of America to arrive at a place of outreach with each other, not to each other. Our common goal was to defeat white supremacy and forces of anarchy.

I had extended the outreach work that inspired me so much, beyond the Muslim community, to building bridges across the diverse landscape of Pittsburgh. This was a gift of Leadership Pittsburgh; a capacity to look beyond my mosque and people, consider myself truly an American, have ownership in what was wrong with my country and do all I could to rectify the harm.

But life goes on and we change places. Our work should not stop but the tide of life takes it to different shores. Just when it looked like life had brought me to a calm place, after a decade and a half of figuring out and making peace with a town that stood true to its blue collar values, it was time to move to a different city. This time, it was Baltimore.

. 10 .

BALTIMORE- 2020

"In the quilt of America, every city has stories to offer. These are Baltimore's."

-Antero Pietila, The Ghosts of John Hopkins

We never decided to move from Pittsburgh. It just happened. Why and how was Baltimore our city of choice? Somehow the stars aligned, and it all came together. On December 27, 2019, in the middle of winter, we moved from Pittsburgh to Baltimore.

We had lived in Pittsburgh for fifteen years. It was our home, a city I had come to see as my own. I enjoyed the familiar convenience of driving through its neighborhoods and alleys, mountains and tunnels, seldom needing a GPS. But, at the same time, Bilal and I recognized that what we called comfort was actually complacency. UPMC Children's Hospital had been a good place for my husband to start his professional journey, but more than a decade down the road, he needed to branch out and take the next step in his career. Another reason for the move was our proximity to the U.S. Squash scene. Both our girls were competitive squash players, and squash was not exactly the sport of choice in the Steeler Nation. Every few weeks, we would travel to the East Coast for squash tournaments, which was one of the main hubs of the game in the country.

After a strenuous interview process, of weighing pros and cons of different cities, we decided on Baltimore. Bilal was to work at the Herman and Walter Samuelson Children's Hospital, part of the Sinai Hospital in Baltimore. We were familiar with the Baltimore and Washington DC area through our past travels. We loved the harbor, variety of ethnic cuisine and local squash opportunities that the area provided. We were to move within six weeks of arriving at our final decision.

We did not take our move from Pittsburgh lightly. Our girls were distraught, especially at the prospect of having to cheer for Ravens instead of Steelers. They had never envisioned themselves in any other place. They had received a bunch of Steelers and Pirates gear as going away gifts from their friends and vowed to wear that to their new school on spirit day, instead of purple and gold. I too had carved out a place for myself in Pittsburgh's landscape with my freelance writing and teaching career. It had taken me years to professionally establish myself as such, and I was not sure how it would all evolve in the absence of any network. A group of close friends arranged a lovely going away party for me, at one of my favorite Asian restaurants, during final days in Pittsburgh. I still get teary-eyed thinking of that day that marked my official departure from the city.

We moved, nonetheless, with a heavy heart, excited at the upcoming opportunities, but at the same time, mourning the loss of good friends and our lovely house and neighborhood in Franklin Park.

I had become such a Pittsburgher, that Baltimore's diversity, at first, struck me as odd and unusual. At a fleeting glance, the city was a mosaic of people of different colors, white, black and everything else in between with their hijabs, kippahs and flowing robes, thriving side by side. Together, they all made Baltimore colorful, adding richness to the local culture and cuisine. There were Black and Asian yoga and spinning instructors at the gym. This was an anomaly I wasn't accustomed to. The city might still be embattling its Confederate past on several fronts, but it had come a long way on race relations. This was evident in the dominant role Black leaders played in the city's governance. For me, Baltimore was turning out to be the America that I had always dreamed of.

The people were different too. The first neighbor I met, swooned when I pronounced "Pakistan" "The Obama Way" with long vowels and a soft k. She told me about the conversations her group of friends had, about learning to pronounce country names like the natives. One of my first acquaintances in the city was a writer of Iranian origin whose husband, to say the least, was a rocket scientist. In Baltimore, in 2020, everyone talked about their politics, without making excuses for it. You could feel the "DC effect" on people's conversations, who discussed everything from local politics to rising tensions between the United States and Iran. The first Friday prayer I attended at the Islamic Society of Baltimore (ISB) introduced Muslim and Muslim leaning candidates for the upcoming city elections. Baltimoreans seemed to be focused on a campaign to oust the two remaining Republican candidates from the Baltimore city council. Such was my new world!

There were also similarities between Baltimore and Pittsburgh. They had both developed as working class towns. They both had been beneficiaries of family philanthropic magnets who had invested in the cities' educational and sociocultural landscapes.

We had decided to bid adieu to the suburbia and live in the city. This was an unconventional choice for the big-house, best-school district-loving folks like us, but Bilal and I felt that we missed out so much in the way of experience by staying away from the city. Many of our well-wishers warned us against that choice, especially given the fact that the city of our choice was Baltimore, which was frequently ranked among American cities with the highest rate of crime. Our daughters, who were thorough western Pa. suburbanites, were concerned that our new residence in the Roland Park neighborhood of Baltimore did not have a garage. They were going to attend The Bryn Mawr School, within walking distance of our house. The school's reputation for progressive leanings and academic rigor played a role in our decision- making as we compared it to other independent schools, splattered across Baltimore. Of course, our Desi genes, which by this time, we had successfully transferred to our older daughter, could not overlook the fact that the school ranked first, in all Baltimore area independent schools. Within a couple of months, I was working at The Bryn Mawr School, as well.

Life had started to come together by March. We had plans for the upcoming spring break. I started working during the first week of March and was supposed to fully come on board after the break. The girls were coming to terms with their new life after a period of adjustment. They appreciated the opportunities to play good squash that were splendid around the area.

During the same month of March, the country went into lockdown. The COVID-19 virus disrupted our lives and changed everything forever.

My first day at work was March 9, 2020. It was marked by a general discord. There were no handshakes, since the COVID-19 virus, or

Corona as it was called, was transmitting through touch. Awkwardness prevailed as I met one person after another at my new job, without shaking hands. Everyone looked consumed with an apocalyptic scenario, during which, we would all have to stay in a "lockdown." A lockdown would not only mean that we would have to work remotely, but also that people across the United States would be socially and physically distancing from each other. In such a world, all businesses and services would have to close down and travel would be limited. It seemed as if our fantasies were flying high as we explored what a "lockdown" could mean.

And then, to our surprise and dismay, it all came true. On my fourth day of work the inevitable happened. It was surreal as we saw schools, restaurants, gyms, offices, entertainment and many other businesses from non-essentials to essentials lock down and close, one after another. In a matter of days, schools and workplaces closed, and started moving to virtual platforms. The malls and restaurants closed, bringing American lifestyle and retail economy to a halt. Places of worship closed their doors and went virtual like many other services. We were all asked to stay indoors and quarantine.

Initially, there was peace and restfulness about the quarantine. It provided our family, like many others, a welcome respite from the craziness of the days. Some dubbed this time, Coronacation. Though we had to be available for online work and school , expectations were much less. We took long walks and biked around our new neighborhood in Baltimore. Our car was not started for days. We sanitized everything and hoarded Clorox Disinfecting Wipes. My ten-year-old found a new hobby in making protective facemasks. Schools switched to distance learning, allowing children to work at their own pace. The world was united by quarantine in a way, it never was before that. The social media provided glimpses into everyone's lives, mostly portraying happy pictures of families cooking, baking, reading and making music together.

But as winter turned to spring and spring gave way to summer, fatigue set in. Our family's hopes of exploring new places and making new friends were crushed by the lockdown. After many years we realized the significance of mosque, as a focal point from where our friends and community life emerged. We did not have any friends in this city, and would not even have any opportunity to make any, given the circumstances. The holy month of *Ramadan* came and went without any socializing or mosque visits. My husband and children, who at one point had grown weary of the mosque, now remembered our time at MAP with fondness. In May 2020, Muslims across North America celebrated drive-through *Eid*, where mosques made arrangements to celebrate amidst the pandemic with car decorations and distribution of sweets and goodies. No one got out of their cars, no one hugged or shook hands. We all regarded each other with suspicion and as a presumptive carrier of the novel COVID-19.

In the absence of mosques, the global pandemic brought the Muslim *ummah* together in strange ways. The first of these was the ability to tune into Friday sermons from the comfort of home. We were no longer restricted by geographical boundaries and could tune into a *khutbah* of our choice. The second unifying factor for the Muslims across the globe was the Turkish Netflix serial, Resurrection: Ertugrul.

The Ertugrul series provided American Muslims, like Muslims around the world, an opportunity to revel in their glorious past. Critics called it the Muslim Game of Thrones. At a time of social isolation, this was the closest thing we could find to *halal* entertainment that mosques and Islamic organizations in America had taken upon themselves to provide. The Turkish language drama serial provided a highly dramatized account of the life of one Ertugrul Gazi, the son of Suleman Shah, who was a leader of the Kayi tribe of

Oghuz Turks. He was the father of the first Ottoman Emperor, Osman I, and considered a patriarch of the dynasty. As COVID-19 raged on, so did Ertugrul's army and revelries in Muslim households around the world. With five seasons, averaging over a hundred episodes each, Ertugrul provided a great pastime, all in the garb of religion. For Muslims around the world, the actors assumed the holiness reserved for warriors and martyrs.

For a few months, Ertugrul and its likes kept people busy. Eventually, the longevity of the pandemic became unbearable. People were losing jobs, businesses were closing, the housing market was artificially surviving on government stimuli, with no end in sight.

The pandemic further exposed systemic inequalities inherent in the fabric of American society. The virus hit harder in communities that lived in close quarters and suboptimal conditions. This group contained a disproportionately high number of Black and Latinx populations. School systems were another marker of these inequalities. While independent schools and affluent suburban districts could seamlessly make a switch to distance learning, there was a real loss of learning for the majority of American children. Another impacted population was that of kids with special needs. As schools struggled with connectivity and online curriculum issues, it took them much longer to recognize the importance of social services that were needed more than ever at this time. Even privileged children like mine, struggled with both distance learning as well as social distancing and never hesitated to remind us how much they "hated Corona."

Frustrations mounted on. People were losing jobs. Some were forced to choose between work or parenting as childcare became unavailable. Many others debated the profit/loss ratios of filing for unemployment or holding on to a few hours that their employer could scrape for them, to ensure future job security. The burnout eventually toppled the whole damn system of prejudice and injustice. Ironically, the very day many states were preparing to ease the lockdown restrictions for COVID-19 turned out to be a day marked by curfews in those cities, as an aftermath of riots and protests stimulated by the killing of George Floyd, yet another Black man, at the hands of a Minneapolis police officer.

George Floyd, a forty-six-year-old Black man, was killed in Minneapolis by a police officer for presumptive use of a fake $20 bill. The officer choked Mr. Floyd to death by sitting on his neck and blocking airflow that constricted his breathing. As the nine minutes video of this carnage went viral over social media, Black Americans and their allies took to streets, protesting against a long history of police brutality and racism. The fact that the news of Mr. Floyd's death came at a time when many of us were still grappling with the absurd and skewed reasoning behind the killing of another young Black man, Ahmad Aubery, exhausted the threshold of Americans . It created an awakening that turned into a national movement.

Baltimore's rich African American diaspora, that comprised 62 percent of the city's residents, was impacted by George Floyd's death at a personal level. It reminded them of Freddie Gray, a twenty-five-year-old Black man, who had died in police custody in 2015 due to critical neck injuries. The city had seen its share of uprising and protests against police brutality at that time, that led to many reforms, including the much heralded "consent decree." In 2020, both the Baltimore city mayor and police chief were Black, which represented the strong role the Black population played in this city's governance. There were still tensions, but in race relations, Baltimore as a city was way ahead than most of America.

It was in Baltimore, at The Bryn Mawr School, that my girls

attended their first conversations on racial injustice and pervasive inequalities in America. They, like myself, felt a little lost in the momentum, trying to find their place among white and Black, as the two groups unpacked centuries of historical baggage. America was in the grip of a consuming passion and unraveling under the presidency of Donald J. Trump.

The year 2020 was also the fourth year of the Trump presidency. The four years have been marked by economic stability, thanks to the good and careful economic measures instituted during the Obama years. They were some of the worst for the people of color in the United States. And when I say people of color, I mean everyone on the spectrum between Black and White. According to a New York Times article, 2018 saw a sixteen year high in hate crimes and racially motivated assaults. The President made and dispensed decisions, spread fake news and perpetuated hateful ideology at the flick of Twitter.

The spread of COVID-19 witnessed the worst consequences of a callous leadership in the United States. It turned a health care crisis into partisan politics, in one of the most medically advanced nations of the world. Earlier, the Republican government tried to hide the threat of COVID-19 and America's preparedness to handle it. When the facts were obvious and could not be suppressed anymore, they tried to scapegoat by placing blame on international forces like the World Health Organization (WHO) and China. As most of the United States dealt with the obvious, the Trump administration quietly made plans to defund the United States Citizenship and Immigration Services (USCIS). Many public as well as private entities were beneficiaries of various government stimuli and the Payment Protection Plan (PPP), but the federal government made a deliberate effort to obstruct legal immigration process by restricting funding for USCIS. The future of many aspiring Americans was put on stake, especially those like my mother and father-in-law, who had already paid thousands of dollars in USCIS application and procedural fees and had been awaiting an answer for more than a year. They were stuck in a limbo between statuses , with no job, healthcare or a place to call home. Once again, like everything under the Trump presidency, the people of color had to bear the brunt of American politics.

It is surprising that in a nation composed mostly of immigrants, how fast most of us forget the time we strived to be part of this great country or the perils of living in America, without a permanent residency or citizenship. More surprising, is the American apathy to immigrants and the value they bring to our nation. Except for a tiny minority of Native Americans, who comprise 1.6 percent of the total American population, the rest of us had made a conscious choice to add our families' name to the legions of this country. Some made that decision hundreds of years ago, while others would like to make it today. But an attempt to create institutional whiteness in America by the Trump administration, was so obvious that even my ten-year-old could decipher it and said one day: "I don't think Trump is against all immigrants. He only likes immigrants who look Whitish Orange."

At a time, when most Americans were scrambling for their own sanity amidst school plans for their children and job insecurity, the Trump administration went further and took another jab at immigration. Most educational institutions in America, including the Ivy Leagues, were making plans for virtual classes during the upcoming Fall Semester. On July 6, a directive of the Trump administration, vowed not to issue or renew F-1 visas, for foreign students in the US, if they were not enrolled in at least one in person class. This decision did not go unnoticed, since it included more than the immigrants themselves. It included huge amounts of revenue that the foreign students brought to the American education system in the form of academic fees much higher than that of the locals. In 2020, there were 400,000 students on visas in the United States, and their inability to return to their schools, would mean huge cuts in revenue not just for the schools, but also the US economy. Harvard and MIT were the first to challenge the new visa rule in a federal court. They were supported by one hundred and eighty other colleges and universities around the country. In a historic move, the Immigration and Customs Enforcement Agency (ICE), was forced to rescind its initial order and allow students to stay enrolled as they were, not affected by any new visa regulations.

Our President, meanwhile, played every card in his pocket to divide and rule. He had not only pitched Blacks and whites against each other, but also minorities across America were not seeing eye to eye anymore. There was a sense of desolation and despair and as we attended one Zoom call after another, on topics ranging from reopening plans for schools to equity and inclusion in society, we all wondered about our place in the grand scheme of things. At this critical moment in history, the American Muslim leadership stepped up to raise the morale of the community and helped make sense of many unanswered questions.

Like most facilities and organizations, American mosques and leadership quickly adapted to virtual platforms. They used multiple social media as well as live platforms for weekly sermons and guidance during pandemic. There was a consensus for once. As masks and social distancing policies divided America, Muslims stood behind their community leadership, who explained the value and instructions for social distancing and quarantine, through religious scriptures. We aligned ourselves with the Black Lives Matter (BLM) movement and many *khutbahs* and lectures were dedicated not only to the support of the oppressed of the society but also to our participation in BLM as a moral responsibility. In these times, the Muslim leadership reminded its community of the contribution of the Civil Rights Act to the American Immigration Act of 1965, which had paved the way to America for people from South Asia and Middle East. Prompted by the events around them, mosques like the Islamic Society of Baltimore (ISB) opened themselves to an assessment of their internal culture, "recognizing and addressing the intra-Muslim racism that exists in the Muslim community." This was a huge step for a Muslim organization.

The Islamic Society of North America (ISNA) provided guidance on celebrating holidays without congregational gatherings. Fundraisers continued to take place virtually, and the organizers were finally freed from making the very tough decisions between serving the chicken or vegetable samosas at their event. Internally, at the mosques, many personal disputes and differences were let go, which was a welcome outcome of social distancing. For once, all the mosques across the United States seemed to be unified in their stance to help curb the spread of COVID-19 and keep the larger communities safe.

As I write these words, the COVID-19 curve in the United States has plummeted and plunged several times. Karens across America have joined our President and continue to fight for their rights, so they do not have to wear masks, at the cost of jeopardizing safety for the rest of us. Confederate statues and monuments are coming down. We still have to see the final impacts, but it has been predicted that all

AMERICAN MUSLIM

efforts to outdo COVID-19, would lead us to a recession worse than the Great Recession of 2008. Several big and small businesses across the country have closed, leaving many entrepreneurs and hourly wage earners unemployed. As the US economy starts taking cautionary steps towards reopening, it has to work with 45.7 million Americans who had filed for unemployment by the second week of July 2020. Many physicians have lost lives to the pandemic, while many others have lost jobs like other Americans, as hospitals lost revenue when patients decided to stay away from care, for fear of contagion.

Today, we all keep our heads down, hold on to whatever work we have and march on in the hope that this too shall pass and we will eventually land in a better world.

Epilogue

"There is only one search: wandering...no dogma and no heresy."

-Mevlana Jalal-ud-din Rumi, Thirteenth century Persian poet
and Sufi mystic

In some ways, my life has come full circle. This year I have turned forty and have officially stepped into middle age, at least according to the Encyclopedia Britannica. I have worked in many roles, acquired top leadership positions and at this point feel as if I am back to the basics. I have found a home, in another city by the sea, thousands of miles away from the place of my birth. A lifelong student of Americanism, I continue my journey on the path, evolving in my small talk as a person who does not own pets, is both allergic and scared of dogs and cannot tell one wine from another.

I must have made some wrong turns on my journey, but as I look at the milestones, I remain unapologetic for all the experiences that I have called life. Each experience has helped me evolve, turning me into the woman that I am today. Along the way I have learned many lessons and may be taught a few. This shall continue. America and I will continue to inspire and learn from each other.

My daughters have been my best teachers, never hesitating to remind me to drop that "L" from salmon as soon as they recognize that I am about to order fish at a restaurant. I have learned to pronounce all our family's names with the right stresses for the American ears and never miss an opportunity for educating if I am ever asked their meaning.

In many other ways, both Bilal and I have found a happy medium, raising our children in an ecosystem that draws on all their identities. Though only time will guarantee results, we have tried to create a space where they could grow to their full potentials socially, emotionally and spiritually. As young adults, they already carry their multiple identities as American Muslims of Pakistani descent, in harmony and not in conflict with each other. At fourteen and ten years of age, our daughters enjoy *Nihari* as much as a good hamburger. One of our family's favorite pastimes is to watch together corny movies and sitcoms, which include Bollywood as well as Hollywood flicks. This year, our family's mutual love has been the Netflix Series "Indian Matchmaking," which gives Bilal and me a chance to reinforce our ideals of an arranged marriage, while the girls enjoy the high drama played by human Cupids.

Over the years, my husband has taken on domestic roles that I abhorred, laundry being a premium one of them. I might not have given up on *shalwar kameez*, but I have definitely developed a better sense of judgement on the appropriate weather and occasion for it.

The year 2020 has been so monumental for us personally as well as for the United States and the rest of the world. Our schedules and relationships apprehensively continue to evolve amidst the global pandemic and I wonder what the future holds for us. Media pundits, from cable television to social media platforms, make predictions that change every day. The future of the workplace, the future of tourism, the future of schools- futurism, or predicting the future has evolved as a profession in times when the unemployment rates in America are at an all-time high, only close to the numbers during WWII.

Personally, I am not interested in futurism. I miss my old mundane life before the pandemic, the busy mornings, a time when there were others around who helped me raise my kids. My girls miss their teachers, the school they attended for two months and people they were just starting to call friends. They miss squash. I yearn to get my life back, go into the office I went in only for four days, visit a mosque in my new town and celebrate holidays with people in flesh and blood. I miss our *chais* together.

With all the money poured into pharmaceuticals and scientific research, when in the world would we have the vaccine?

The pandemic has given a new meaning to the word community. It has defined how a community's value is intrinsic and not external. A community is governed by a set of values and shared beliefs and not by physical spaces. However, our need or at least my need, to exist as part of my community is real. At some point, we might have underestimated the value that a *masjid* brought to our family's lives and we cannot wait to meet new friends in our new hometown, at another *masjid* picnic.

There are questions that loomed over us even before the global pandemic, but are now more important than ever, after the failure of leadership that Americans have witnessed in 2020. I wonder if the Trump presidency would continue for another four years after the 2020 election. If it does, what would it mean for the non-white Americans? I fear a scenario in which our communal sense as Americans would disappear, and we would revert to a tribal culture of warring factions, this time defined by our ethnic and culture makeups. Today, many of us try to find hope in the nomination of a Black woman with immigrant parents, as the Democratic choice for the Vice President of America. I wonder if children like mine, and many others of many other colors, would find advocates for themselves in our elected representatives.

My years of leadership for the American Muslim community have given me to constant speculation about our community's future in America, as well as in geopolitical events. We continue to evolve, learning, educating, laughing at our mistakes and our own jokes. Our youth continues to fight for its rights, to exist fully and completely, as American Muslims. Their struggle for the freedom of expression is not only from the conservative America but sometimes, also from their own mosques.

What would be the future of female leadership in our mosques? Would they continue to be delegated to making food arrangements, while their male counterparts make decisions in the board rooms? Would organizations like MAP have more women presidents, or Muslim women, like many other American women, would continue to survive under comfortable patriarchy?

Would the United States of America ever embrace a woman president?

I hope, one day, Insha Allah!

RESOURCES

1- Aslan, Reza. *No God but God: The Origins and Evolution of Islam.* Ember, 2012.

2- Curtis, Edward E. *Muslims in America: A Short History.* Oxford University Press, 2009.

3- Hartford, Margaret E. *Allegheny County's Americans by Choice: Descriptive Material about the Foreign Born of Allegheny County.* American Service Institute of Allegheny County, 1944.

4- *Institute for Social Policy and Understanding.* www.ispu.org/.

5- Pietila, Antero. *The Ghosts of Johns Hopkins: The Life and Legacy That Shaped an American City.* Natl Book Network, 2018.

6- Pew Research Center, Muslim Americans: https://www.pewresearch.org/topics/muslim-americans/

7- Toker, Franklin. *Pittsburgh: A New Portrait.* University of Pittsburgh Press, 2009.

GLOSSARY

(In alphabetical order)

Allah

> God

Allahu Akbar

> God is the greatest. This phrase is recited by Muslims in many different situations. For example, when they are very happy, to express approval or during times of extreme stress.

Amma

> Mother

Aqiqah

> Aqiqah is the Islamic tradition in which a baby's head is shaved as a cleansing ritual and an animal is sacrificed and its meat distributed among the needy to ward off evil eye.

Barelvi school of thought

> A majority sect of Islam in India and Pakistan.

Biryani

> An Indian/Pakistani dish made with rice and meat.

Bhai

Brother, friend- used as an expression of friendship.

Chai

A South Asian method of preparing tea steeped in milk.

Chand raat

Night of the Moon. It usually refers to the night of moonsighting for the first of Shawwal, to celebrate Eid al-Fitr.

Desi

A term commonly used to describe a person of Indian, Pakistani or Bangladeshi origin. *Plural:* Desis

Diwali

The Hindu festival of lights.

Eid

Eid in Arabic means feast, festival, holiday. Muslims celebrate two Eids during an Islamic calendar year. Eid al-Fitr is celebrated at the end of Ramadan and Eid al-Adha is celebrated during the last month of the Islamic calendar.

Eidi

Eid gift which mostly consists of money.

Gora

A white/Caucasian man. *Female:* Gori

Hadith

Record of the traditions or sayings of the Prophet Muhammad

(PBUH), revered and received as a major source of religious law and moral guidance. Muslims consider hadith second only to the authority of the Quran, the holy book of Islam.

Hafiz

A person who has memorized and can verbatim recite the entire Quran.

Hajj

The pilgrimage to Mecca in Saudi Arabia. Hajj is prescribed for all Muslims who have means to undertake the pilgrimage, at least once during their lifetime.

Halal

Arabic for permissible. Halal food is that which adheres to Islamic law, as defined in the Quran.

Halaqa

A religious gathering or meeting for the study of Islam and the Quran.

Hijab

In common usage, hijab is a veil worn by Muslim women which usually covers the head and chest. The term can refer to any head, face, or body covering worn by Muslim women that conforms to Islamic standards of modesty.

Hijabi

A woman who wears a hijab. *Antonym:* Non-hijabi.

Hindi

One of the official languages of India.

Holi

 The Indian festival of spring.

Holy Quran/ Quran

 The holy book or scripture of Muslims.

Huqqa

 A water pipe.

Iftar

 The meal eaten by Muslims after sunset during Ramadan.

Imam

 The person who leads Muslim prayers.

Insha Allah

 If Allah wills it.

Islamophobia

 Prejudice or hatred against Islam and/or Muslims.

Jazāk Allāhu Khayran

 May God reward you [with] goodness. An Islamic expression of gratitude.

Jihad

 Struggle, effort.

Khutbah

 Sermon.

Kitty parties

Kitty parties are a popular way in some parts of Asia for women to socialize within the context of an informal savings club. Kitty refers to the amount collected at the party, every member contributing a certain sum of money each month. The kitty is handed over to one member of the group every month.

Masala fries

French fries sprinkled with Pakistani spices.

Masha Allah

What Allah/God has willed - Used as an expression of appreciation, joy, praise, or thankfulness for an event or person.

Masjid/ Masajid

Mosque/ mosques

Mithai

Sweetmeat, dessert.

Muslimah

Muslim Woman

Nihari

Curry/stew consisting of slow-cooked meat, mainly shank meat of beef, lamb or mutton, along with bone marrow.

Nikah

Marriage contract in the Islamic law.

Pakora

Fritter made with gram flour. It is a fried snack and popular street food.

Quran/ The Quran

The central religious text of Islam, believed by Muslims to be a direct revelation/word from God.

Ramadan

Ninth month of the Islamic calendar, observed by Muslims worldwide as a month of fasting (*sawm*), prayer, reflection and community.

Salah

Ritual prayers for Muslim.

Salafism

The Salafi movement developed within Sunni Islam in Al-Azhar Mosque in Egypt, as a response to Western imperialism during the late nineteenth century.

Samosa

Fried or baked pastry with savory fillings, such as potatoes, onions, peas, cheese, meats or lentils.

Sawab

(Arabic) Reward.

Sehri/Sahur/Sahoor

The pre-dawn meal consumed early in the morning by Muslims before fasting.

Shaitan

The devil, demon, evil spirit.

Shalwar Kameez

A traditional combination dress worn by women, and in some regions by men, in South and Central Asia. Shalwar are trousers which are typically wide at the waist and narrow to a cuffed bottom. The kameez is a long shirt or tunic. The side seams are left open below the waistline. The combination garment is sometimes called shalwar kurta, salwar suit, or Punjabi suit.

Sharia

An evolving and diverse sect of moral principles that govern Muslim family and penal laws.

Shawwal

Tenth month of the lunar Islamic calendar. It follows Ramadan and is marked by the celebration of Eid Al-Fitr on the first day of the month.

Shukriya

(Urdu) Thank you.

Subhan Allah

(All) praise be to God. Used as a general expression of praise, gratitude, or relief.

Sufism

Islamic mysticism.

Sunni Muslim

Sunni Muslims are the largest denomination/sect of Islam. The tradition is followed by 80–90% of the world's Muslims, characterized by a greater emphasis upon the traditions of the prophet and his companions.

Tableegh

Proselytizing.

Taraweeh

Extra prayers which Muslims observe at night in the month of Ramadan.

Ummah

The entire Muslim community, that is bound together by the concept of Pan-Islamism.

Urdu

Official language of Pakistan.

Wahhabism

A puritanical and rigid form of Sunni Islam.

Yarhamuk Allah

May Allah have mercy on you. Said to a person who has just sneezed.

Zabiha

Meat slaughtered according to the Islamic rulings. *Antonym:* Non-zabiha

ACKNOWLEDGEMENTS

This book would not have been possible without three men, who each contributed in their own way, to make me the woman I am today. My late grandfather, Abbajan, who imbibed me with the love of learning. My father, Abu, who taught me, by example, to never compromise on principles. And my husband Bilal, who always encouraged me to follow my passion.

A less acknowledged but ever-present and supportive person in my life is Faizia Sitwat, my mother-in-law. A children's author herself, she has been there to help me raise kids, attend graduate school and help run the home during the final days of finishing this book. Her care has come in various forms during the years, from babysitting her grandchildren to cooking two meals a day, when all of us hunkered down at the house for months, during the COVID-19 pandemic. If it was not for her help, the publication of this memoir would still be a figment of my imagination.

I would be amiss if I don't mention my greatest cheerleader in life, my Ami. Ami always encouraged me to push my boundaries and excel in all pursuits, from school to homemaking and motherhood.

Many thanks to Patti Rickert-Wilbur, Library Director at The Bryn Mawr School for reviewing the manuscript and being part of my writing process. I am indebted to Mila Sanina for perfecting the manuscript in a way that only she could. I appreciate the thoughtfulness and guidance of my editor, Meg St-Esprit McKivigan.

The more I know about life, I realize how blessed I am to be part of a close-knit family. My brothers, Rehan and Nauman, sisters-in-law, Sarah and Naaelah, continue to fill our Pakistan trips with joy and excitement. They act as untiring translators for my children and help me navigate all things I left behind in Pakistan many moons ago, from street addresses to haggling with the tailors while getting new shalwar kameez stitched.

Finally, I must acknowledge my two lovelies, Sabina and Alina, who wish they did not find themselves subjects of my writings so often. I am inspired to do good in the world and leave it a better place for my daughters and nieces, Ayla, Iraj, Miraal and Shanaya. The future belongs to my girls!

Made in the USA
Columbia, SC
16 September 2021